can it be true?

can it be true?

a personal pilgrimage
through faith and doubt

Michael Wakely

Foreword by George Verwer
former international director of Operation Mobilisation

Kregel
Publications

Can It Be True? A Personal Pilgrimage through Faith and Doubt

© 2002 by Michael Wakely

Published in the United States of America in 2004 by Kregel Publications, a division of Kregel, Inc., P.O. Box 2607, Grand Rapids, MI 49501, by permission of Inter-Varsity Press, Leicester, England.

ISBN 0-8254-3944-2

Printed in the United States of America

04 05 06 07 08 / 5 4 3 2 1

Contents

Foreword

I would not be writing this if I had not learned a long time ago that great faith is not in the absence of doubt, but so often in the midst of it.

Mike Wakely is a disciple of the Lord that I have known for over thirty-five years and a person for whom I have very high respect. He has spent much of his life on the 'frontlines' in Pakistan and it was a privilege to be with him there on different occasions.

Several words come to mind as I read this book:

- *Reality*: these pages have a powerful ring of reality. True stories of real people, not all with happy endings, jump off the pages of this book.
- *Honesty*: this is so very important in these days. As you read this book you will be moved by Mike's openness and honesty.
- *Faith*: for me, the life of Mike comes forth louder than words in this unique book. As you take the time to read it, and I hope you will, then you will catch something of the faith of this man who has walked with God these many decades.

For those like myself who also struggle with doubt, this book is a huge help and blessing. As I turned the pages of the manuscript and also thought of Mike and the greatness and the mercy of God, there was a leap of hope and faith in my heart. As I read of God's working in Mike, I burst into tears.

This book gives the clear challenge that we don't have to have answers to all our questions before we can experience salvation and the reality of faith. God is here and we can know him and experience him and his great salvation.

George Verwer

Introduction
What's the point?

This is a book about faith – to be specific, the Christian faith – not a book of doctrine and dogma, as many such books might be. What I have written is the product of a personal pilgrimage, as much for my own benefit as for anyone else's. The fact is that, in my experience, faith has always walked hand in hand with doubt.

When I told someone (who has known me for years) that I was writing a book about doubt, she looked at me with astonishment. 'I didn't think you had that sort of problem,' she said, suddenly seeing me in a new light. Another friend, when he heard about what I was writing, thought I was passing through a spiritual crisis and needed help. Maybe I do. But, if so, it has been a spiritual crisis that has lasted for more than forty years.

My great desire in writing has been to be honest – in my experience, a rare and difficult quality. Honesty can be threatening and dangerous. It can also be extremely helpful.

As I write these chapters I have several different kinds of people in mind.

The honest struggler

First of all I think of many honest and committed Christians who want to be authentic in their faith but still struggle with questions that find no easy answers. While writing I had an email from a close friend, who said: 'My main problem is over the idea that somehow God has left the issue of heaven, hell and salvation entirely with the preaching of the gospel. At university we used to say rather glibly to intelligent non-believers that the fate of those who had never heard was not our problem. But that doesn't really add up.'

In my understanding, doubt is not a sin, nor is it a failing. It is a mark of an intelligent and authentic faith. Faith that never asks the hard questions – and by implication never tackles some honest doubts – is often not genuine faith but an artificial imitation without a very deep foundation. Yet isn't it crucial to have ready answers – not standard clichés but reasonable solutions – before doubt turns into unbelief? This is why my book is intended for honest strugglers.

The disillusioned sceptic

Then I think of those people who, in their words, have 'tried the faith' and 'found that it doesn't work'. There are more of them around than we dare to imagine – people who started out well with excitement and genuine conviction, but then found church boring and irrelevant, and their deeper questions unanswered. I had a letter some years ago from a young woman who worked with me for a year in mission work in Pakistan. She committed herself to an intensive 'ministry of prayer'. Her letter told us that, after many years of trying hard, she had decided 'it doesn't work'. She was therefore writing to tell us that she was no longer a believer. She moved away and didn't send us her new address. I hope she will pick up this book somewhere and read it, because I believe there are genuine answers to honest questions for those who want them.

The cynical critic

Finally, it is possible that this book might have something to say to the cynical world that has assumed the Christian faith to be fairy-tales for the gullible, obscurantism that bypasses the mind. Such are so often the assumptions of otherwise intelligent people today. People delight to prop clay pigeons on the fence and then take pot-shots at them. My hope is that we will present, not superficial, but authentic images that intelligent people will be more able to grasp and believe in.

The cynics who have discarded religious formalism, tradition and boring piety have my sympathy – especially if they have been hurt by accompanying moral judgmentalism! Some Christians are quite good at all of that. But the critics are in danger of throwing out the baby with the bath-water. They make a tragic mistake when, in a desperate quest to satisfy an inherent spiritual passion, they turn instead to Eastern religions, romantic pantheism or simple licentiousness, which make no moral demands and just require people to do what comes 'naturally'. I can understand the dilemma, but believe it to be fatal. After all, a jelly without a mould will make a horrible mess on the table. Such feelings often conceal a cry for authenticity, and need pegs and markers that have some link to reality.

1

Faith in Context
Mosquitoes in the living-room

I have often wondered why God made mosquitoes. They seem to serve no useful purpose, unless to provide a meal for certain birds, though that is small compensation for the trouble they cause.

When I lived in Asia for a number of years mosquitoes were my constant enemy. I grew used to devising methods to keep them away – creams and oils, smoking coils and blue tablets that gave off anti-mosquito fumes. I sometimes slept under a mosquito net, though I discovered that some mosquitoes are really clever and can get inside the best-sealed net. They then are trapped and can enjoy an uninterrupted feast. I even tried a specially designed whistle that was supposed to deceive mosquitoes into leaving me alone.

One of the more ingenious methods was an electric mosquito swatter, with wires that were charged by a small battery. Swat the mosquito, and it would be electrocuted as it touched the wires. It worked! Sparks could be seen as the mosquito made contact with the wires, and the little critters would fall crumpled to the floor. I remember, however, one evening as I was preparing to go to bed. The bedroom was buzzing with mosquitoes, so I set about leaping around the room and dealing fatal blows to my little enemies. After some time I realized that, however many I killed, for some reason the number of mosquitoes was not diminishing. Something was wrong. It was then I discovered the problem. My electric mosquito swatter was not killing the beasts but simply stunning them. They fell to the floor and after a few dazed minutes they revived and took to the air again – to be swatted once more as soon as I could get to them.

That is a picture of my lifelong battle with doubt.

I have been a Christian for a long time and cannot question the authenticity of my experiences of faith and my commitment to Christ. I have seen answers to prayer and some amazing 'coincidences' in my circumstances that are best interpreted as supernatural interventions. Yet for every affirmation of God's grace, a question mark has flashed in my mind – like another mosquito buzzing in my ear – to tell me there is another side to every story. I swat it with my built-in faith-charged problem-solver, and the little beast falls to the ground, lies there dazed for a few moments and then revives and returns to plague me with doubt once more.

Credentials

Before I go too far into my grand subject, I think it is helpful to give my credentials. After all, who wants to read a book about doubt that has been written by an unbeliever or a novice? The fact is that I am not an unbeliever, nor an agnostic. Nor am I a triumphalist who pretends to have all the answers. I don't want you to feel you are being conned – I am, and expect to remain, a committed believer in God and Christ. This faith is what makes me swat mosquitoes.

My conversion in 1962 was a radical and life-reorienting moment for me. I was a third-year language student in Trinity College, Dublin. Having had a middle-of-the-road churchy background, I knew the basics of the Christian faith. More than that, in fact, I had already had some unusual spiritual experiences even before I had any deep personal faith. My mother was crippled by polio in 1950 and could only walk with the help of a stick and a calliper in her shoe. Then in 1956 she was miraculously and suddenly healed. There was no question of the authenticity of the miracle. Mother bounced back to a full and active life. I tell the story in a later chapter.

In university I did my best to prove that God didn't exist, because I found it inconvenient to believe in him and still enjoy myself with all the range of things that students like to do. I wasn't specially keen on parties and alcohol, nor did I do anything particularly bad, but God was still an inconvenience I could not afford to consider. There was a certain logic to this thinking for which I am grateful. I reasoned that, if God existed and the Bible was true, then that would have to be of supreme importance. Every other value in life would pale in comparison. If one is to believe in him at all, this must logically become an absolute allegiance.

The crisis came to a head when I moved into college rooms with one of those over-committed zealots who are best avoided if you want a peaceful lifestyle. I never realized the move would be so embarrassing or risky. Steve was also studying Modern Languages. I knew he was religious but was not ready for what happened next. Within days he had Scripture texts all round the walls, which I had to apologise for whenever my friends visited me in my rooms. 'Stephen is a religious nut,' I would mutter.

Then one Sunday afternoon he sat me down for a Bible study. I had to humour him, but I hardly understood a word of what we studied – the Gospel of John, chapter 1. Before I knew it, I was designing posters for a forthcoming college 'mission', which I was then obliged to attend. John Stott was the preacher, his theme: 'Behold Your God'. I still have the posters I prepared.

My logical leap of faith

All of this time I was being backed into a corner. I could no longer afford to ignore the logic. Either I had to turn my back on the whole idea (which increasingly looked like moral and intellectual cowardice), or embrace it with all my heart and soul. I did the latter, getting down on my knees in my little bedroom and yielding my life to Christ as best I knew how. The results were startling.

For the next few weeks I walked on air. A whole range of fears and anxieties had been replaced by an inner happiness and certainty that I had never known before. For reasons that are hard to explain, the Christian faith suddenly made sense. A multitude of complex jigsaw pieces had amazingly fallen into place. I could no longer understand why the whole world did not follow suit and embrace Christ, and I spent hours arguing with my pagan student friends. Late in the night after the library closed, we would sit down over coffee in some dingy college quarters and discuss the logic of faith into the early hours. They were heady days. None of my old friends was convinced. None of them followed my logic and gave his life to Christ.

For me, however, it was but the start of the great adventure. After I had got over the early euphoria and discovered that there was a lot still to learn and perfection was not just around the corner, I quickly grasped the new direction my life had to take. If I had committed myself to God because that was the logical thing to do, then logically he had to be the focus of the rest of my days also. What we used to call 'full-time service' clearly had to be my future. In my understanding at the time, that implied some kind of ordained ministry, though later developments took me on a different course.

The purpose of my telling this is not to give my personal history, but to detail my credentials for writing a book about faith. The point I want to make here is that my faith has not been simply an academic exercise or the adoption of a routine inherited from my parents. It started, and it has continued, with some very convincing experiences of divine intervention in my life.

After graduation and a year of recovery, when I juggled with thoughts of going to Africa as a teacher with the Rwanda Mission, I spent two years in Bible College in the conviction that every building that will stand must have a foundation. I found the study of theology intriguing and much more fascinating than its dusty reputation suggested. But I learned much more than good theology from some fine teachers. Probably the greatest lesson that I gained from those two years was the disappointing complexity of some Christians in community. Far from being heaven on earth, as I had in my naivety expected, I found Bible College a hot-bed of charismatic controversy, carnal ambition and small-mindedness. It was a valuable lesson.

In 1967 I went to India with a missionary movement called Operation Mobilisation. To be honest, I have always been slightly embarrassed by the name, but I have got used to it. The sixties were exciting years – the beginnings of the Vietnam protest movement, CND marches, the Beatles and youth rebellion. I mercifully bypassed the political protest agony and the drop-out society. We were Christian idealists and had dreams of taking the world for Christ, not for some political or moral ideal.

I was inspired and driven by the example of C. T. Studd, who said: 'If Jesus Christ be God and died for me, then no sacrifice can be too great for me to make for Him.' I was also attracted by another young radical, George Verwer, who was propagating a message of forsaking all for the cause of world evangelization. Operation Mobilisation (OM for short) was the organization he founded in the early sixties in the belief that, if the gospel was true, we owed it to the nations to tell them about it before they slipped into eternity in ignorance. It attracted a lot of idealists for all sorts of good and bad reasons.

The world is almost twice as large now as it was then – world population has doubled in the past 40 years – but there were a lot of non-Christian people even then, and somehow we imagined that we would succeed where generations of missionaries and evangelists before us had failed. I had my doubts about that, but doubt has always existed alongside faith in my life. After I had been in India for a few months I had gained an unfortunate reputation as a negative thinker, and George Verwer sent me a book with the title *The Tough-minded Optimist*, in the hope that it would make me less critical and more positive.

(I later discovered that he had not carefully selected the book to meet my needs, but had in fact picked up several hundreds of them as a remainder for sixpence a copy. But I enjoyed reading it anyway.)

I lived and worked for seven years in India, for three years on an evangelism team made up mainly of Indians, and then in various office and administrative positions. We lived very simply and made many sacrifices and, on the whole, loved it all. Meanwhile I had got married, and Kerstin joined me in this lifestyle. In 1974 the government of India decided that we were undesirable and we moved to Nepal. Two years later the government of Nepal also decided we should move on.

In 1979 all the signs pointed Kerstin and me to what we now look on as the most significant period of our lives, in Pakistan. We arrived in Lahore in October, followed a few weeks later by a mixed team of inexperienced young men and women, to begin the work of OM Pakistan. This is not the place to tell the story of all that followed, but suffice it to say that they were years of fulfilment and failure, success and struggle. We made many mistakes, but the end result has been a growing and substantial work, now under national leadership.

As we go through this book I shall draw many of my illustrations from the years in India, Nepal and Pakistan. My purpose here is not to be autobiographical, but to give some credence to my commitment to Christ and to provide a context for the struggles of faith that this book is about.

The apostle Paul said in his last letter to Timothy: 'I have fought the good fight ... I have kept the faith.'[1] I still have a long way to go. I cannot say, 'I have finished the race', as Paul did, but I can identify with many of his other statements. Even he had his struggles and failures. He was afflicted and perplexed, 'but not driven to despair'.[2] He too had cause to be anxious and at times to question. But in the end he was able to affirm: 'I have kept the faith.'

So be it.

2

Cerebral Faith
The cost of thinking too much

A few years ago there was an outbreak of unusual phenomena in some churches in Britain. It started in South Africa, moved to Canada and from there came to Britain, becoming known popularly as the 'Toronto Blessing' because of its wholesale adoption by the Airport Church in Toronto. People travelled from all over the world to Canada to experience the phenomena, and then brought back the 'blessing' to their own churches. So it spread. In church after church people claimed to have been touched by God – blacking out, falling on the carpet and acting as though drunk. I describe some of my experiences with the Toronto phenomena in a later chapter.

Like many Christians, I was fascinated by the blessing and had no desire to miss out on something the Lord might want to give me. And yet my mosquitoes started buzzing. I discussed my doubts and questions with a trusted friend.

'You know what's wrong with you, Mike,' he said. 'Your faith is too cerebral.'

I have meditated on those words ever since, wondering whether he had given me an insight into my big problem, or had unwittingly given me a compliment. In reality he was telling me – 'Mike, your problem is that you use your mind too much. Your mind is blocking what God wants to do in your life. Shut down your brain and your faith will revive.' The more I think about it, however, the more I believe that he was complimenting me on something I should be very grateful for.

The Bible has a lot to say about using our minds. Jesus commanded his disciples to 'love the Lord your God with all your ... mind',[3] and then 'opened their minds so they could understand the Scriptures.'[4] It is stating the obvious to say that the mind is useful, but there are Christians who advise that it is only when we shut down our minds that God will be able to take over. That's just what the critics of Christianity have been saying for years: Faith is intellectual suicide.

John Stott states in his helpful booklet *Your Mind Matters*: 'If we do not use the mind which God has given us, we condemn ourselves to spiritual superficiality and cut ourselves off from many of the riches of God's grace.'[5] I like that. God has given us a mind, and expects us to submit it to him and then use it. Our minds are there to search for good answers to the hard questions – and if those answers are still not satisfactory, to have the wisdom to submit in faith to the certainty that there is a superior wisdom above.

A faith that invites investigation

One of the marvellous qualities of the Christian faith is that it is not a closed and sealed box; it is open to intellectual investigation. Christianity does not require a blind leap in the dark, but urges a faith that examines, studies and reaches sound conclusions, and then invites the cynics, the questioners, the intellectuals and the thinkers to come and do their best. The Christian faith says to the world: 'Examine me. I have answers that are intellectually satisfying as well as emotionally appealing. I have nothing of which to be ashamed, nothing to hide. In fact I have better answers to some of the big questions than any other philosophy can satisfactorily provide. Come and investigate.'

I recently studied an Open University course on sociology. In our opening tutorial we were each asked to give a short personal introduction of ourselves. I told the class who I was and what I did in life. After the hour was over two or three people asked me, with some astonishment, why I was studying sociology. 'They will teach you all sorts of things that are against Christianity. Why did you choose this subject?' I replied, 'If my faith can't be questioned, it's not worth having. I believe my Christian faith can stand up to examination.' Are Christians only supposed to study theology?

The popular conception is that the Christian faith requires closed eyes and closed minds, followed by a surge of comfortable feeling. As long as the feel-good factor is there, the irrational leap is justified. That is a travesty of a faith that is rooted in space, time and history. I have lived long enough with other great world religions to know that there are other ways of looking at faith, which do not invite close intellectual examination. But it is not so with Christianity.

Nor is it true to say that the rational approach is just a 'Western' concept and that Eastern religions have a different – even a superior – appeal. The plain fact is that few world religions invite examination under the microscope and prefer, or even claim, to be regarded either as a mythology, because they deal with abstract concepts rather than concrete realities, or as above inspection, because examination is viewed as an insult to the divine.

It is unfortunate when Christianity is judged in the same light, and the impression is given that one needs to turn off the mind in order to believe – 'Choose faith or brains, you can't use both together.' Or 'Close your eyes, submit yourself to your emotions. God is an experience to make your feelings tingle. Switch off your brain before it gets in the way.' Sadly, a lot of Christian teaching – and even more Christian experience – would agree with these popular travesties.

The Bible and true Christianity have been urging people to use their minds for centuries. It is therefore a compliment to be told that I have a 'cerebral faith' if it means that I exercise my brain to understand and order my relationship to God and the world.

More questions than answers

Now, having said all that, I might sound very brave and convinced. But I am not. I am still a coward at heart with more questions than answers.

The second time I ever preached in the open air was a disaster. The first time was also a disaster but there were not too many people around to understand me – it was in Brussels market and I was speaking in poor French. How did I ever dare?

The second time was at Speakers' Corner in Hyde Park in the summer of 1965. I had a friend who used to go into London every Sunday afternoon. First he would go with his soapbox to Hyde Park and then on to Westminster Chapel to listen to 'the Doctor' – Dr Martyn Lloyd-Jones. One Sunday he invited me to join him and I agreed. I had no idea he was planning to put me on the box.

To all would-be preachers I strongly advise you not to start out your career at Speakers' Corner. I was about eighteen inches higher than the sea of heads around me and looked out on the crowd, wondering how to start. I launched into some sort of personal testimony. Within minutes I was heckled.

Hyde Park is a meeting-place for the professionals. Sure enough, out there in my audience were several professional hecklers, who get their fun every Sunday from setting out to destroy young religious zealots, like me, with difficult questions. The secret (which I discovered afterwards) is to totally ignore them. I was stupid enough to be distracted by them and then to try to answer their questions, and was very quickly demolished. I stepped down from the box humiliated and a little wiser.

I am still slowly learning to be wise. The first great thing to learn is not to be afraid of the questions. If our faith is valid and strong enough to last, it must be ready to be questioned. The apostle Peter encouraged his readers always to 'be prepared to give an answer to everyone who asks you to give the reason for the hope that you have'.[6] That takes courage.

The second great lesson to learn is that we must never give up the search for good answers. The Bereans 'examined the

Scriptures every day to see if what Paul said was true'.[7] We may never get adequate answers to all the questions. But we must never give up trying. Some questions may only have answers in eternity. As limited humans we are bound to end up in some frustration and tension – learning to grapple with what is unanswerable. The mind that examines and believes also questions and doubts. That is where we admit mosquitoes into our living-room.

The third great secret is to grasp the importance of perspective. Many of our problems exist because our perspective is so limited. We are like bugs crawling across the forest floor, trying to draw a map of the world. With our finite minds we seek to grasp infinite realities. To think and understand with the mind of God is difficult – but mercifully not totally impossible, because he has let us in on many of his secrets. That is where the Bible comes in and takes such an important role in our quest for a good mosquito swatter.

I would love to have written a triumphant book of affirmation – easy answers and quick solutions are so much more appealing – but real life is not like that. I have read Christian biographies that relate a succession of miracles, a triumphant progress of faith from seed to maturity. I have drawn lots of encouragement from such tales, but cannot say that it has been like that with me.

Doubts derive from many quarters, don't normally arrive in any sequence and are quite unpredictable. In real life questions don't come in tidy queues or neatly packaged. They sometimes come in swarms and life is a battle for survival. At other times, mercifully, they don't appear and we can sail through a day on wings of confident faith.

Is God really there?

This is my most fundamental doubt. Even though I have made God the centrepiece of my career, I admit that I still have some difficulty with the very concept of the supernatural in a rational age. It is a doubt that is *socially* derived. Much of Western society now assumes that science has abolished everything it cannot see and touch and experiment with, and puts enormous pressure on its citizens to conform. Whether the media sets the pace or follows the trend, this is the message they drive home with monotonous arrogance: all unusual phenomena must have a rational explanation, and those who believe otherwise are made to look foolish. It makes some sense. Surprisingly, as we shall see, waves of superstition and a wistful longing for spirituality are battering at the shores of rationalism in a brave irrational leap, popularly known as post-modernism.

Why be so narrow?

When I accept the phenomenon of God and the reality of the unseen world, I am then faced with another problem, which seems to arise from a *moral* source. Spirituality is one thing, but true spirituality is closely allied to both dogma and morality. Why is it necessary to be restricted to such a narrow definition as is required by Christianity? We live in a pluralistic society. Does it not make for good sense and communal harmony for everyone to believe what he or she wants to believe? Why be so narrow as to think that Jesus and the Bible are superior to others, or even unique, in their access to truth? This is not an abstract question. Who does not struggle with the boast that everyone is wrong except a small number of Bible-believers? Life would be much simpler if we could all work out our own versions of the truth.

The ground of truth

It is tempting to bypass the problems of the Bible in a volume of this nature, because the questions are so complex. I love the Bible and I read it every day. Some of it I find dull and difficult and some of it is inspiring and helpful. There are passages that the whole world needs to know and follow, and there are other parts that frankly embarrass me. Why on earth does God think we need to know about the inheritance of Zelophehad's daughters?[8] Even Martin Luther had his problems with the letter of James – a book I actually find rather helpful.

These difficulties are mainly *intellectual* and need to be addressed accordingly. There are more questions here than we can adequately attempt to examine in a volume of this size, and we must defer to other scholarship and present no more than guidelines to survival techniques. But be sure of this – with confident answers to the problems of the Bible's inspiration and authority, the solution to everything else is relatively straight-forward. Chapters 4, 5 and 6 deal with those issues.

How can I be so weak?

Perhaps one of the difficulties that forces me to question the reality of my own faith more than anything else is disappoint-ment with myself. These are problems that often arise from the *emotions*, but are no less devastating. I claim access to absolute truth in Christ, so why am I so timid about it? I profess to believe that I am a party to the power of God, that 'incompar-ably great power for us who believe',[9] so how can I be so pathetically weak in so many ways? When I speak for myself I speak for the church. There is such a dichotomy between what we Christians profess and the way we behave, that it makes me wonder whether our profession is really genuine. I am sure the world wonders too.

Multiplying mosquitoes

My questions and doubts stretch much further than this. (You may have other questions that don't particularly trouble me.) And those mosquitoes come at us from every quarter – from our *intellects* and our *emotions*, from *society* around us and from our *disappointed idealism*. They come from the *dichotomy* between claim and reality, and *disillusionment* with our own behaviour as well as with that of other Christians. I know that suffering is a huge problem for many people. How can God be good and still allow his creation to suffer? I do not actually find that such a problem, but I have included a chapter on the subject because it is such a stubborn thorn for many. I am more troubled by the difficulties presented by the promises of God and unanswered prayer ... or the unfairness and injustice of a world where some have so much and many have so little ... and the immorality of a world hurtling towards the abyss while the people of God make daisy chains.

Yet, in spite of all the doubts and questions, I am a believer, and probably the stronger for having put my faith to the test.

Roy Clements is a troubled Christian leader who has been transparent about his struggles, and he has offered us some of his wisdom about faith and doubt:

> The only sort of faith that is immune from that kind of questioning is a blind faith, a faith which dare not look the realities of the world in the face, a faith that has to close its mind off to anything that threatens its creed. That is an irrational faith, a cowardly faith. It is a faith that fully deserves the contempt of the sceptic for it confirms that believers are just pathetic weaklings who need a crutch of faith with which to limp through life. But real faith isn't blind; real faith doesn't shut its eyes to evidence that seems to contradict its convictions; it can't do so.[10]

This confirms my conviction that authenticity can afford to be examined under the microscope. If it fails the test, it was not worth having anyway. If it passes the examination, it will be ready to face yet another trial. For every answer that I have discovered to life's great questions, I usually find myself faced by further questions. The stunned mosquito not only revives, but gives birth – and then calls for reinforcements.

I have met a few people who have managed to survive with an unquestioning faith, and I admire their serenity and strong convictions. Occasionally I have got myself into trouble by sharing my doubts with friends, who immediately assumed that I am on the verge of heresy or apostasy. If you are one of these, untroubled by doubts, I admire you and apologise for sharing my struggles.

An important distinction

Before I conclude this chapter, there is an important clarification I must make. I looked up 'Doubt' in a Bible dictionary, and was pointed to the article on 'Unbelief'. That is probably an unhelpful reference. The two are very confused in many people's minds, but they are worlds apart. 'Unbelief' translates two New Testament words, both carrying implications of rebellion and disobedience. An 'unbeliever' should be avoided by believers because they have nothing more in common than Belial and Christ.[11] 'See to it, brothers,' warns the writer to the Hebrew Christians, 'that none of you has a sinful, unbelieving heart that turns away from the living God.'[12]

It has to said that doubt, left unanswered and feeding on the cynical encouragement of the world, can easily lead to unbelief – active rebellion and moral disintegration. Sadly, we have all seen it happen in the lives of once faithful believers. But in itself, doubt is a different matter altogether from unbelief. Biblical doubt is better seen as perplexity or uncertainty. As the women were 'perplexed' when they stood before the empty tomb on Easter day[13] and Paul was 'perplexed, but not in despair',[14] so the crowd that witnessed the extraordinary events of the Day of Pentecost were 'amazed and perplexed'. They asked one another, 'What does this mean?'[15] They needed guidance. They needed answers.

Roy Clements offers more insights:

Contrary to popular myth, doubt is not the opposite of faith. To suggest it is, is to confuse doubt with unbelief, whereas doubt and unbelief are, in fact, two quite different things. If you think about it, doubt is something only a believer can experience, for you can only doubt what you believe. Doubt is to unbelief what temptation is to sin. A test, but not yet a surrender.[16]

If you are a thinking person, most likely you also have some perplexity that could do with good answers – or at least pointers in the right direction. It is not good to sweep such dust under the carpet – or, to keep the analogy, to try to go to sleep with the mosquitoes buzzing about your head – because sometimes those doubts will not just keep you awake, but sting you to death.

3

Where on Earth is God?
Is religion relevant?

I once risked an honest confession with a mature and enthusiastic believer whom I looked on as a close friend. I thought he might be sympathetic and could possibly even help me. I cornered him in a hotel lobby at a conference we were both attending. 'Do you ever struggle with doubt?' I asked.

'Yes, I do,' he answered. It was a promising start.

'I have constant doubts and questions too,' I continued, hopeful that we were getting onto the same wavelength. 'What do you find most difficult?'

'I find it difficult to believe how God can really love me.'

What a correct answer! I thought. Just the kind of problem that every good Christian is supposed to have, because it both gives honour to God and credits us with humility.

'You know, I have more fundamental doubts than that.' I tried again. 'I sometimes wonder if God exists at all. Do you ever have that problem?'

My friend looked at me aghast. I had obviously crossed a line in his mind between believer and apostate and I quickly got the message that I had better back off before he mentally packed me in a box with 'reprobate' on the label. I retreated and quickly re-established my reputation as an orthodox evangelical. But the doubts remain and I find it hard to believe that I am alone in fighting this giant mosquito.

Please do not misunderstand me. As I have said at the

beginning, and I hope my credentials demonstrate, I believe in God. When I stand in church and recite the creed I do it with all my heart and absolute sincerity. The bottom would truly fall out of my world if I did otherwise, as I have staked my life and career not only on God's existence but also on all that flows from it. And I actually do believe what I say.

But it is a belief that our modern age finds increasingly quaint and irrelevant, and which needs to be demonstrably authenticated if it is to survive and be taken seriously.

Stand up! You're all alone

I am clearly not unique in sometimes questioning where God is in my world. Western society functions on the assumption that we are alone. Francis Schaeffer called it a 'closed system'. If God exists at all, he doesn't appear to intervene very often in his world, and at best we need to give him token acknowledgment as the One who wound up the clockwork mouse and let it free to run till the spring has uncoiled. Ever since the dawn of the Enlightenment, people have played safe with the assumption that science and reason contain all the answers to our problems, and if you want something done it is better to go ahead and do it rather than wait for a divine intervention. God has been displaced in his universe.

BBC television showed a series of programmes late on Sunday nights entitled *The Soul of Britain*. It examined the religious state of the nation, drawing many of its conclusions from an extensive survey of the values and beliefs of the British conducted at the end of April 2000. The results were fascinating – but perhaps not at all surprising:

- 62% said they still believed in God.
- 69% believed they had a soul – 5% more than 10 years ago.
- 52% believed there is some form of life after death.
- 31% considered themselves to be 'spiritual'.

In contrast to this, only 26% believed in some form of personal

God and only 23% thought that the Bible was the unique Word of God. Significantly, 71% believed in sin and only 8% called themselves 'atheist'.[17]

Michael Buerk introduced the second programme with the sort of questions that must sometimes cross every thinking person's mind: 'Has science swept religion aside? Have religious beliefs been reduced to nothing more than superstitions we would be better off without?'

Here is the comment of Danah Zohar, a philosopher asked for her views about God. It is pretty typical of many confused and thinking people:

> If you ask me if I believe in God, I would be very confused what to say. I know I believe deeply in a fundamental sort of root of being, that there's a ground of being, that there's a deep self. And yet, if you ask me if I believe in God, I wonder what do I say to her, because am I then putting myself in the camp of those people who believe in some old man in the sky or a personal God? I don't believe in those things.

Such people have a point. The point seems to be one of massive confusion and it reflects the normal 'enlightened' view of the vast majority of people around us – rationally conditioned, superstitiously entrenched and nostalgically wistful. I have to confess that, though I am not nearly as confused or afraid of confessing belief in a personal God as Ms Zohar, I too struggle with the reality of God in everyday life.

My questions run something like this:

If God is really there, where is the evidence for his existence? The 'God of the gaps' is no longer needed. Human ingenuity and scientific expertise have demonstrated that many natural phenomena no longer require the postulate of God to explain them. And if he is there, is he relevant and still required for daily life, or can we get on just as well without him?

Sometimes a clever preacher will say, 'If the Holy Spirit went away – or if God died – what difference would it make to your life?' or words to that effect. I think it is a silly question, like saying: 'If

you take the source of life out of us, what difference will it make?'
The answer is obvious: 'We will die.' But I also think the question
contains an element of truth. So much of life is dependent on rituals
and routines. The absence of God might change my lifestyle in the
long term – less church attendance and probably less optimism about
the ultimate future of the world – but everyday realities would go on
much as before.

In fact, distressingly, there is little difference in lifestyle between
those who profess to have a personal relationship with the eternal
Creator God and those who live good, clean, middle-class, pagan
lives. It is a very troubling thought.

Alternative choices

There is no doubt that Christian belief in the existence of a
personal God, 'the Creator of heaven and earth', is under fierce
attack today, undermined by the relentless insinuations of the
media, poorly represented by its adherents and made to look
trivial by the public spectacle of its professional representatives.

Some years ago I attended the enthronement of a bishop in
one of our wonderful cathedrals. It was an extraordinary and
elaborate ceremony, and I counted it a privilege to be there, a
significant moment in the dedication of a Christian leader.
The extensive ritual focused on the man in extravagantly
embroidered robes under a decorated mitre. The spacious gothic
building echoed with the formal chant of the choir. I wondered
how it would have been if he were dressed in a suit and tie and it
had taken place in a church hall.

What, in heaven's name, I thought, does this ritual have to do with
real life? It has more to do with history and tradition than with
everyday reality. It typifies the status of religion in the contemporary
world – an irrelevant relic from the past. It gives small comfort to
realize that I have the same thoughts when I watch the Trooping of
the Colour on television, or the changing of the guard at Bucking-
ham Palace. Splendid but irrelevant.

On the other hand, formal atheism – the claim that we are really alone and capable of keeping our own house in order without outside help – has been equally thoroughly discredited by the war-torn history of the twentieth century. Scientific materialism receives no credit from a bleak era that threatened, in Winston Churchill's famous words, 'a new Dark Age made more sinister, and perhaps more protracted, by the lights of perverted science'[18] and by the cruel failed philosophies of materialistic Marxism.

It must be said that the European mood of cynicism towards traditional Christianity is not typical of the world as a whole. The picture is very different in America, where religion thrives and polls claim that no less than 90% have a faith in deity of some kind. In the non-Christian lands of Asia and Africa such polls are deemed irrelevant. 'For Hindus, Muslims and Sikhs, their religion is still central to their daily lives,' said *The Daily Telegraph*.[19]

Even in cynical Britain in our so-called post-modern age, belief in spirituality and an unseen world is actually experiencing a revival – even while the masses turn their backs on any kind of formal religion. A recent book confirmed some interesting trends among British teenagers:

> Almost as many teenagers believe in ghosts and horoscopes as believe in God, according to an extensive new survey.
>
> While 41 per cent said that they believed in God, 40 per cent said that they were convinced that ghosts existed and over a third – 35 per cent – put their faith in the veracity of horoscopes, the survey of 34,000 13 to 15-year-olds found.
>
> Nearly a third of those questioned thought it possible to contact the spirits of the dead, two out of every 10 believe that fortune tellers can see into the future and 22 per cent believe in black magic.[20]

Superstition is thriving in our scientific age. The *Star Wars* films both reflected and moulded our culture. David Wilkinson, a Fellow of the Royal Astronomical Society and a Christian apologist, wrote this of his fascination with *Star Wars*:

Star Wars unashamedly introduced spirituality into its central themes, such as hope, the battle between good and evil and the fact that there is more to the Universe than just that which science can describe.[21]

Star Wars defined the popular mood – an instinct that there is more to life than cold science can define, and a rejection of the dogma, the tradition and the morality of orthodox religion. It was just what people wanted, a religion where everyone could feel good about themselves and believe in a divine energy to suit their own needs. Wilkinson quotes a letter to *The Guardian*:

What *Star Wars* fans are so eager to embrace is the supernatural currency lost in modern bureaucracies – the magic of fantasies, transcendence and just plain mystery.[22]

My mother died in February 1977, shortly after the book *Life After Life* by Raymond Moody[23] had been popularized by the *Readers Digest*. The book purported to be a serious study of near-death experiences and to demonstrate from interviews with people who have returned from the brink that there really is an existence beyond the grave. Moody's investigations sought to reveal that, after a person dies, he or she experiences a period in a dark tunnel and then exits into a blazing light. Some who have had near-death experiences have claimed that they encountered a figure of light, accompanied by feelings of peace and an unwillingness to go back to earth. It was all very comforting and he was taken seriously by many Christians. The book was an instant sensation. It touched the popular mood.

I am almost ashamed to confess it today, but I derived comfort from the pseudo-science of Raymond Moody and the similar writings of Elizabeth Kubler-Ross, author of *On Death and Dying*.[24]

Kubler-Ross ultimately became a practising spiritualist, involved in the occult and 'out-of-the-body' experiences, and her work was largely discredited. But she too had demonstrated a point. There is a longing in many people – including myself – for evidence of the supernatural and life beyond life. My shame is that, as a practising

Christian, I ever took them seriously. I have much greater evidence of the supernatural – and of life beyond death – in my own experience of Christ and my grasp of the Bible's teaching.[25]

There is truly a God-shaped void in our hearts.

Making sense of the confusion

Incredibly, our heads continue to fight against the instincts of our hearts. Battered by the propaganda of the day, spiritual survival depends on finding convictions that satisfy our minds while fulfilling the cry of our hearts. One of the blessings of today's cynicism about religion is that we are forced to examine the authenticity of our beliefs.

In the midst of popular confusion and like a rock rising out of the turmoil, the Bible has some extraordinarily up-to-date parallels to draw. It is arrogant to view today's world as significantly different from that of Bible times. Of course, at the level of scientific understanding and discovery there have been huge advances, but human instincts and morals have not changed very much, nor has human behaviour. The world of the Old Testament sounds surprisingly modern, with its confusion of superstition, idolatry and practical unbelief. Listen to the cry of the psalmist:

The fool says in his heart,
'There is no God' ...
The LORD looks down from heaven
on the sons of men
to see if there are any who understand,
any who seek God.[26]

Like a stubborn crag in a swirling torrent, the lonely prophet stands out in the midst of this social indifference and denounces the follies of the day:

When men tell you to consult mediums and spiritists, who whisper and mutter, should not a people enquire of their God? Why consult the dead on behalf of the living?[27]

An opinion poll in the ancient Middle East might have revealed very similar statistics to those of our modern age. What is so impressive is the courageous stand of the few, like Isaiah, who stood up against the tide and continued, to their everlasting credit, to proclaim the impeccable existence of a righteous deity. That gives us hope. The majority is not always right – indeed, the majority is usually wrong!

This is not the place to give comprehensive reasons for my continued faith in God. Many books have been written that give evidence for his existence, examining creation and science. Many of them are convincing and helpful. But let me outline a few further thoughts – apart from the affirmations of Scripture – that have helped me cling to faith in the midst of the questions. The more you look, the more you find. The important thing is never to stop looking.

God in miniature

The BBC showed a series entitled *Alien Empire*[28] in 1996 in which they peered into the amazing world of insects. Let me quote from the first episode in the series:

> Humans think they own this planet, but they have only been around for a couple of million years. This world belongs to insects and it has done so for 400 million years. Possibly 30 million different kinds – more than the rest of the animal kingdom put together.
>
> Each and every insect is a perfect miniature machine. They wear tough waterproof armour that protects their soft insides and supports their body – the best design for their miniature world. Insect design goes far beyond heavy-duty engineering. They also perfected micro-architecture.
>
> The most sophisticated flying insect is the humble housefly. Its wings are powered by special muscles that contract at very high frequencies, up to 500 times a second. They produce enormous amounts of power, weight for weight similar to a

small aircraft piston engine, and its flight path is controlled by an onboard computer that makes the latest electronic designs seem primitive. It flies on one pair of wings. The hind pair are reduced to knobs that act like gyroscopic stabilisers.

It was an astonishing programme as a whole, but most astonishing for me was the repetition of the word 'design' – the 'design miracle' of the insects and the incredible 'design innovation' when insects 'evolved wings ... No-one has any idea how this happened. The earliest fossils had fully formed wings ... Insect wings evolved from scratch, completely new structures. No compromises here – just infinite design flexibility.'

How can our age be so blind – struggling with the design miracle and yet refusing to acknowledge the Master Designer! An article in *Time* magazine on 'the greatest works of art on the planet' – underwater colour and design in marine life – stated this:

> Says Lily Honegger: 'Nature is the artist,' one with such creativity that on each reef and in every sea, 'the landscape is different, the colours are different and the species are different.'[29]

In two pages that describe the inventiveness of an astonishing Designer, God receives no credit. Of course, the BBC and *Time* are delivering political correctness for public consumption and this is repeated throughout the media. It is quite acceptable to attribute the works of God to 'nature' or 'evolution', but quite wrong to give God any mention – even where creation is stamped with the Maker's trademark.

I am aware that this argument is by no means conclusive and is in general discredit nowadays in academic circles. There are clearly other possible explanations for the remarkable intricacy and order of the universe. Sir Martin Rees, Astronomer Royal and 'one of the greatest cosmologists of his generation', though fully aware of the astonishing design of the universe, and the extraordinary suitability of the earth for human habitation, nevertheless does not presume on the existence of a Creator but believes that 'the anthropic principle selects this universe out of many' for human habitation.[30] We can take our choice.

David Wilkinson concludes wisely: 'None of these things prove the existence of God. However ... we do see things that are certainly consistent with and for many people suggestive of a creator who wills the universe to bring forth life.'[31] For me, I am still bowled over by the incredible complexity and wonder of the grand design of our world.

Sunrise in the soul

I think the most splendid sight I have ever seen was the sun rising on Mount Kanchenjunga in the eastern Himalayas. It was a winter morning in 1973 and we were staying in Kalimpong, a hill town north of Calcutta. We were there for a conference, but took advantage of the opportunity to appreciate the beauty. I was never a great enthusiast for nature and rarely took time to just stop and stare, but I got up early that morning and climbed up Tiger Hill, from which, we were told, we would have the best view of Kanchenjunga. It was worth the effort and it broke through my indifference to beauty.

The air was cold and there was a heavy mist in the broad valley that separated us from the next mountain range. And then the sun slowly rose and touched the tip of the snow-covered mountains with its pink rays. The mighty Kanchenjunga was suddenly a towering golden mass, rising up out of the mist in the valley. It was the most beautiful sight I had ever seen, and though it is now thirty years later and I have seen many other mountains, I still remember it. Such a sight is impossible to describe adequately, however clever I might be with the English language. Why?

The appreciation of beauty touches something inside us that materialism cannot match, a value that is inexplicable and yet one of the marks of our humanity. It does not prove the existence of God, even if it demonstrates the qualities that cry out for him. Nor does it even prove the reality of a spiritual world, though it touches the borderline of what we understand by it. It does, however, illustrate that we are not talking nonsense when we speak of a quality that is super-material. The Bible comes close to explaining it when it says: 'The heavens declare the glory of God; the skies proclaim the work of his hands.'[32] The hardened materialist looks foolish when he describes the experience of beauty as no more than a programmed chemical reaction.

C. S. Lewis spoke of this indefinable quality in terms of 'Joy', an experience beyond words, which demonstrated without need of further explanation that he was more than flesh and blood. We have all had those experiences. We may call them instincts, or second sight, or perhaps just feelings. But they override every question about the existence of a spiritual value in life.

For Lewis this Joy was the tremor that proved the existence of the reality beyond itself, in itself exhilarating, but in itself no more than an indicator of an ultimate truth. In the battle between Joy and the occult, Lewis found nothing to compare to the purity and wonder of Joy:

> Two things hitherto widely separated in my mind rushed together: the imaginative longing for Joy, or rather the longing which *was* Joy, and the ravenous, quasi-prurient desire for the Occult, the Preternatural as such ... This ravenous desire to break the bounds, to tear the curtain, to be in the secret revealed itself, more and more clearly the longer I indulged in it, to be quite different from the longing that is Joy.[33]

That experience is much more than an appreciation of beauty. It is the unseen and the intangible making itself known in the human psyche. Who can explain the atmosphere in the streets of London on the eve of Princess Diana's funeral? Could it be diagnosed in a laboratory?

Inside the wardrobe

The Lion, the Witch and the Wardrobe is one result of C. S. Lewis's discovery of Joy, as well as one of the world's great children's stories – never out of print, widely translated and adapted for television and theatre. *The Lord of the Rings* was voted the best book of the twentieth century by thousands of its adult admirers, propelled into another world by the stretch of Tolkien's imagination. J. K. Rowling's Harry Potter books have topped the best-seller lists and are likely to remain very popular for a long time to come. What is it that makes these magical tales (and their accompanying screen adaptations) so popular and so able to catch the public imagination?

Is it that they have touched a raw nerve in materialistic, scientific mankind by introducing the magic of another world into the mundane? Who is not fascinated by the thought that possibly, just possibly, there really is a world of magic and mystery that lies at the back of the wardrobe, or on Platform $9\frac{3}{4}$ at King's Cross Station? The theme is as ancient as humanity, and holds out an enduring fascination for generation after generation. What does this tell us about ourselves? Do we love the world of Narnia, and the world of Hogwart's School of Witchcraft and Wizardry, where good and evil are sharply contrasted, because that is a world our human nature yearns for?

I haven't attempted to 'prove' the existence of God in this chapter. No proof can ever be produced that will do more than convince the person who wishes to be convinced. Nor does the Bible itself ever try to prove the existence of God. It assumes his reality and calls anyone who denies it a 'fool'.

But I have, I hope, made some inroads into the good sense of clinging to faith in a spiritual reality beyond the senses, in the midst of a thousand conflicting doubts and questions. In fact, when I begin to look at the world around me, I find it makes a lot more sense to believe in a divine, invisible realm than not to believe. There is more, much more, to life than what I can see and feel and taste. God has left his fingerprints everywhere.

It is the next question that actually presents much greater difficulties. Christians claim that 'the Force' – the world behind the wardrobe door – has shape and is knowable. But there is a price to be paid by those who want to know it, the price of accepting what it (or he) will reveal about itself (or himself). That is what separates our culture's contemporary 'spirituality' from true Christianity.

4

Finding Your Way
Has God really spoken?

When I first trusted Christ I received enormous help and encouragement from members of the Dublin University Christian Union. One of the finest was a student called Richard. He was not brilliant and was struggling his way towards a general arts degree, but as a friend he was warm, approachable, open and honest. When I was timidly finding my way into Christian circles, he was the sort of person who made me feel welcome. His love for the Lord was infectious.

I had another good friend in the Christian Union named Simon. He was a total contrast to Richard. He bore himself like an aristocrat, spoke wonderful Queen's English, and was clear, concise and succinct. I thought he would make a good Church of England vicar. His theological convictions were likewise well formulated and convincing. Once I had broken the ice I found he had a heart of gold.

After graduation, our close company scattered, but we kept in touch. Richard, sadly, had a nervous breakdown, to no-one's great surprise. For all his warmth and friendliness, he was emotionally unstable. I visited him in the psychiatric hospital in Virginia Water in Surrey, where he was undergoing treatment. He was visibly troubled, but still full of the Spirit and love for God.

I went away to Bible College and then took off for India, and we were no longer in regular contact. But then out of the blue I received a letter from Richard.

He and Simon had somehow linked up – like chalk and cheese – and together had come to the conclusion that God was speaking to them about the imminent destruction of the world. The two of them had begun to travel around Britain warning people that God's judgment was imminent and it was time to repent and flee to safer ground. The reason for the letter was to plead with me to join them before it was too late. They felt God had told them that I should join them in Northern Ireland, which they thought would be spared from destruction.

Now, what was I to do with that? 'God has told me...' he wrote.

God has told me...

That's a big claim. But it lies at the heart of one of the greatest problems in our knowledge of God. If there is a God up there – or in here – how can we be sure who he is? Francis Schaeffer, a theologian and apologist for the Christian faith, wrote a book entitled *He is There and He is not Silent*. It is a complicated book, but the title says it all. A God who exists but doesn't communicate would be a God we could never get to understand or know. We are in the dark unless he speaks.

But here my dilemma deepens and it needs some good answers.

The world is filled with voices, and many thousands claim to be the voice of God. How in heaven's name can we know what to listen to? Even among Christians there are contrary claims about how God speaks and what his words mean. My friends Richard and Simon told me that God had spoken to them. Should I trust that claim and follow regardless? Or were they deceived?

Another close friend, with whom I studied in Bible College, wrote to me from Nigeria. He is an outstanding Nigerian Christian leader, for whom I have always had the greatest respect – and still have. In his letter he said, 'God has told me that you should come to Nigeria to work with us.'

'God has told me...' How am I to know that it is God speaking to me?

After the American presidential election of November 2000, Bill Clinton made this memorable comment: 'The American people have spoken, but it is going to take a little while to determine what it is they said.' God has spoken; how can I determine what he has said?

For those brought up in the Christian tradition, it is natural to accept that God's Word is to be found in the Bible – that what he has to say to us is to be found in the pages of the Old Book. We will look much more closely at the nature and contents of that book in the next two chapters, because it raises many questions. Here we want to focus more closely on the question of whether that is all that God had to say. And that too raises many questions.

How should we understand those who claim 'God has spoken to me'? Do we need to be satisfied with an ancient book? Or can we expect something a little more up-to-date? Has God said all that he has to say and left us to try to work out what it means? Has he been silent ever since the first century? Or can we expect more immediate help? Is it irrelevant to listen in the hope that God might have a special word for me? If God is alive and loves me, I want him to say something to me!

Does God still speak today?

I well remember an invited teacher coming to speak to our team in Lahore. With a dramatic gesture he took his Bible and laid it on one side, with words calculated to disturb our small world: 'We used to think that this was how God spoke to us – through his Word, the *Logos*. But now [a dramatic pause] ... God is speaking into the here-and-now through his living Word, the *Rhema*.' Apart from presenting us with some poor exegesis (the two words for God's Word are used more or less interchangeably in the New Testament), he was deliberately trying to shock us into thinking more deeply.

We were only a small group and the teaching did us little harm – and perhaps some good. He was highlighting a popular fad, and being deliberately provocative. Partly due to the hushed respect that traditionally has been given to the Bible, it has become trendy to downplay its importance. Popular preachers sometimes claim that Christians worship God the Father, God the Son and God the Holy Scriptures – which may sometimes be too close to the truth to be funny. So now they swing to the other extreme.

It has become fashionable to regard the Old Book as musty, dusty and out of date. Who wants to live in the quaint pages of history when there is an alternative? Behold, the *NEW* has come! New is good, old is dead. It is a snare that wise people need to be wary of, especially when it comes to God's revelation to us. In that case, the old is definitely not dead, and the new is often dangerous.

If only we learned the lessons of history! During the Reformation, a man by the name of Thomas Müntzer mocked Martin Luther for his addiction to the dead letter of the Bible. He nicknamed Luther a 'Bible-gobbler' and proclaimed: 'It is of no use to have swallowed the Bible one hundred thousand times,' to which Luther replied: 'Müntzer, I wouldn't believe you if you swallowed the Holy Ghost, feathers and all!' The emphasis of Müntzer's religion was prophecy and the fullness of the Holy Spirit, and he led a movement that added controversy to confusion over the question of how God speaks to his people today.

The question of prophecy

The exercise of spiritual gifts has been, in some people's vocabulary, one of the 're-discoveries' of biblical truth in recent years, and 'Spirit-filled' believers are now expected to be 'moving in the gifts' of the Spirit, as detailed in 1 Corinthians 12.

No-one can confidently deny that the gifts of the Spirit are biblical and were in common practice in the New Testament church. I don't personally believe they were rediscovered in the last hundred years. I think they have been in evidence throughout church history, but perhaps less dramatically highlighted. Thomas Müntzer certainly thought so too. But the greater emphasis on the gifts in recent years has surely been healthy and helpful to many. Nevertheless it has provoked controversy.

Prominent among the gifts is the gift of prophecy. God has assured us that one of the signs of the last days would be that 'your sons and daughters will prophesy, your young men will see visions'.[34] Paul picked out prophecy as a specially important gift for the church.[35] I have lost count of the times I have heard someone stand up in the middle of a church service to proclaim with a dramatic air: 'Thus saith the Lord: Behold, I am doing a new thing ...' or something similar. And I admit that occasionally these 'prophecies' have the ring of truth, come true or point very personally and very relevantly to a particular need. Surely God does on occasion speak to his people directly today.

But the Bible is as full of warnings against false prophets as it is of examples of the genuine gift. The warnings have often been unheeded in the scramble for the spectacular and the exciting.

How should we relate the written Word of God to this spoken word? It is one thing to conclude that God has spoken in the Bible – it is another altogether to believe that he is adding to that body of truth through spoken prophecy. The potential for confusion is immense. In other words – back to the first question – how can I know what God has said? And be sure that it is true?

At an evening service some years ago when my wife and I were being commissioned to return to Pakistan, a group of church elders gathered around us, laid hands on us and prayed. After the prayer we prepared to return to our seats, when one of the elders took me aside. 'I feel the Lord wants me to say this to you: "Beware of him, who claims to be one of you, but is no part of you."' I was left with this mystical 'word' which I dared not forget. I could not afford to ignore it in case it was from God.

It put me in considerable difficulty. If that was a true 'prophecy', I had always to be looking out for some kind of traitor in the midst. God might have told me that one of my co-workers was a wolf in disguise. I needed to be suspicious and on my guard. In reality, in the coming months I encountered several people who fitted the description. One or two of them caused me considerable harm. But that is the normal expectation of Christian ministry, and the Bible has given us adequate warnings to look out for them.

To this day I can see no special usefulness for that 'word of prophecy', and I finally concluded that it was an imaginative piece of rather unhelpful advice dressed up in 'prophetic' terminology. I find that quite distressing. For anyone to claim to be speaking on behalf of God ('Thus says the Lord . . . ') is an audacious thing, often taken far too lightly. It can cause a lot of confusion if taken seriously – and a lot of disrespect if ignored. God's word is not to be taken lightly. Christian people have tragically trivialized it, and even risked superseding it with exciting alternatives.

However passionately I may long to hear God's personal message whispered in my ear – and believe me, at times I have longed for that experience – it is absolutely essential to be convinced that the Bible is God's unchangeable statement of truth against which all other standards must be judged. The margin for error is so broad when every Christian claims the right to speak for God in prophecy, that we must tread very carefully when we take such pronouncements seriously.

Hindrances to truth

What a treacherous path we tread if we cannot even agree among ourselves what that truth is! While claiming exclusive ownership of absolute truth, we go to war with one another over trivial issues of doctrine and practice – such as the validity of using guitars in worship and the wearing of hats in church. Talk about straining a gnat and swallowing a camel!

If we Christians had a clearer conviction about the source of our authority – if we could agree exactly how God speaks to us and what it is he has said – and if we spoke with a united voice in the midst of the general confusion, we would perhaps sound more convincing.

Interpretation and conviction

Some find safety in clinging to the authoritative interpretation of the church, while others launch out on an individualistic journey of self-discovery and sometimes unearth surprising and unorthodox things along the way. There is, of course, validity and value in both approaches, which is why the world is so full of denominations and sects, all of which think they have made an exclusive discovery they cannot live without. And the Christian church continues to disagree over whether there should be sixty-six or eighty-three books in the Bible.[36]

Experience and practice

There are sects that can only baptize 'in the name of Jesus', others that must have running water and full immersion, and those that won't baptize at all. There is an African sect that feels it is biblical to jump, so all its members jump as they worship. Some dress up in elaborately embroidered uniforms, while others can only wear white. Others must bring soap – or candles – to church. It would not be quite so bad if we were less serious about our differences, but some of us will go to war to defend our distinctive habits, because we believe God has told us to practise them. No wonder we are confused.

Subjective and objective

'It feels so right', 'I have the inner witness in my heart that it is true', 'I really felt the Lord was in it', 'I have such peace and joy', 'God has told me ...' and so on – expressions of those who wallow in experience. On the other hand is the cold focus of those who glory in total objectivity with or without personal engagement. As science-fiction writer Philip K. Dick said: 'Reality is that which doesn't go away when you stop believing in it'[37] – truth regardless of experience. So who is right, who reflects biblical truth?

I was listening to an interview on BBC radio some years ago. A breathless and enthusiastic young lady was telling how her life had been transformed and she had found deep peace and joy in her life. I listened intently, happy to hear a Christian testimony on the radio. It wasn't what I thought. After some time she admitted how excited she was to be a part of the Hare Krishna movement. Contrast with this enthusiasm the testimony of those who can argue blindfolded on doctrine and dogma, but whose experience of God is as warm as a block of ice.

How can we know what to believe?

This is beginning to look increasingly like a maze with no clear way through – or to keep the analogy, a mosquito-infested jungle. One possible reaction, which is as tempting as suicide for those who are disgusted with the confusion of the church, is to give up, to conclude that truth is and always will be impossibly illusive. I prefer to cling to the conviction that there has to be a more effective mosquito killer. So in conclusion, I want to outline a few attitudes that I believe are essential to hold onto in our search for truth. Ignore the guidelines and the mosquitoes will quickly sting us to death.

The need for humility

Humility is an elusive quality. The moment you think you have it, you lose it. But a humble mind is essential if we are to come close to truth. In this context, by humility I mean the ability not to believe that we are infallible, however clever we may be, and the willingness to accept what might initially appear to be unacceptable, and to believe things that look incredible – such as the centrepiece of the Bible, that the eternal Creator became a human being. If God has spoken, it is the humble mind that is able to hear what he has said. The arrogant will be looking in the wrong direction and so will miss it.

Charity and patience

There are few Christians who agree absolutely on every point of doctrine, but on certain things we must agree. There are fundamental truths that are essential if we are to remain credibly Christian. 'Anyone who comes to [God] must believe that he exists and that he rewards those who earnestly seek him.'[38] By definition a Christian believes in the existence of God, and the same may be said of a number of other truths that are essentially non-negotiable: the reality of human sinfulness and our need of salvation; the righteous law of God and his justice; the impeccable sinlessness of Jesus the Son of God; his atoning death and bodily resurrection, and so on.

But beyond those essentials, there are many doctrines and practices that we can agree to differ about. If someone wants to worship God by jumping, though I feel no need to leap, I see no reason why he or she should not. In my understanding, the same is true of methods of baptism, gifts of the Spirit and a lot of other Christian teaching and practice.

Endless vigilance

God surely does speak today and we need to be endlessly sensitive to hear what he has to say. But he has given us a standard by which to judge what he has said, and that is in his unchanging and unchangeable Word. God has sometimes spoken to me by highlighting a truth from the Bible, but at other times he has spoken in my inner mind, through another Christian or a book. I know he speaks in dreams and visions (the Bible tells me so), though most of my dreams are so bizarre that I am personally very hesitant to attempt an interpretation. God speaks in gifts of prophecy, words of knowledge and in the interpretation of tongues.

But vigilance is essential. Our own hearts deceive us so easily, the devil is out to blind us and lead us astray, and discernment is needed more than any other spiritual gift. Thank God for a standard by which to judge what is true and what is false, the standard of the written Word. It's not out of date at all. It is as modern and relevant as today's newspaper – and a great deal more reliable.

Every truth is surrounded by lies, every true prophecy is met with a counterfeit. The Bible urges us not to be so stupid as to believe every word or every 'sign'. 'Dear friends,' wrote the apostle John, 'do not believe every spirit, but test the spirits to see whether they are from God, because many false prophets have gone out into the world.'[39] The claim to possess all the truth – even when we call it the 'Full Gospel' – is an arrogant claim. Such self-assurance is an open door to deception. Greater humility and greater vigilance are surely the requirements for safety in this slippery world.

Truth and love

F. F. Bruce, a respected teacher of the Bible, commenting on some passages in the writings of John, said, 'He who does not love is not just a bad Christian. He is not a Christian at all.' It is a bold statement, but no bolder than what John wrote in his first epistle.[40] That means that, if I am so convinced that I have the truth that I despise those who disagree with me, I have immediately lost my claim to the truth.

In contrast to this is the opposite mistake of being so loving that we welcome every heretic and false teacher. The one who wrote so much about love also wrote: 'If anyone comes to you and does not bring this teaching, do not take him into your house.'[41] Truth and love are essential companions and must walk hand in hand in mutual respect.

5

So Many Books
What's so special about the Bible?

My first encounter with Hinduism was in the early 1960s when I travelled to India with a team of other zealous young people. On arrival we teamed up with some Indian Christians and sallied forth into the villages and bazaars with boxes and bags full of Bibles and Gospels.

Our attitude to Hinduism, as we understood it, was typical of many Westerners – amazement that anyone in the twentieth century could still believe such fables and myths. How could anyone in this rational age still make a religion out of the colourful pictures of the Hindu gods and actually bow down to worship them? Hinduism looked like a house of cards that was ready to collapse as soon as the logical light of the gospel shone upon it. We went forth to distribute books of apologetics, which clearly set forth the logic of the Christian faith. They should have caused people in their millions to abandon their traditional ways and put their faith in the truth. Or so we thought.

But, amazingly to us products of rationalism, devotees to Hinduism continued to increase in numbers and to grow in fervency. Our logic failed to dispel the myths. In fact, in many ways the myths and the fantasies seemed to be conquering, even if much of it was fuelled more by a pride of identity and a rejection of imperialism than by conviction.

I studied the life of Swami Vivekananda, a Hindu spiritual

leader of the nineteenth century who had attempted to reconcile Eastern spirituality and Western thought. Then I obtained a copy of the *Bhagavad Gita* in an attempt to understand the philosophy that so gripped millions of Indians.

It was the early 1960s and Calcutta was in the grip of Marxist enthusiasm, fuelled by the Cultural Revolution that was sweeping China. Slogans covered the walls all over the city: 'Power comes from the barrel of a gun' and other revolutionary sayings of Mao Tse-Tung. For a few *paise* I bought a copy of the *Little Red Book* – the thoughts of Chairman Mao. It was called the Marxist 'bible' and millions tried to live by its teachings.

And then I was given a copy of the Holy Quran, the sacred book revered by millions of Muslims.

The world is full of books and teachers who all claim to be the Ultimate Guide and to present the True Path. And I am no less convinced that the Bible is the Word of God. It raises many crucial questions. Why am I a Christian (rather than a Hindu or a Muslim) and how can I be sure that the way I follow is true?

The Muslims are equally convinced – and often much more convinced than we Christians – that their book is God's final message to the world. They are sure that the Bible has been superseded by the Holy Quran, and that the Quran is the truth. The Bible, important as it was in its time, has been changed and is unreliable – so they say. Why should I believe that my claim is superior to theirs?

There are many books that purport to guide us into the unseen world. If I am going to put all my eggs into one basket, it would be good to have convincing and clear evidence that my basket is reliable. Maybe other baskets hold more eggs or will protect them better.

It would be so much easier to believe that the Bible presents just one of many ways to God – which is what many people believe today. But it is a hollow claim for anyone who still believes in truth. Either salvation is solely through Christ (as the Bible claims) or it is exclusively through Islam (as Muslims claim). Or they are both wrong and some other path is the True Way. All cannot possibly be true. Or can they?

The sterile debate

There will be no end to the claims of Christians and Muslims, and those of other religions, as to which has the *best* Book – the *true* Book. It has become popular in some circles to arrange debates where scholars from conflicting religions hold a formal debate in public. The end result is invariably sterile.

Ahmad Deedat was a Muslim debater from South Africa, who delighted to take on Christian theologians in debate. He had two great secrets. Firstly he would ensure that his audience was overwhelmingly Muslim and therefore in his favour, and secondly, he would make sure that he could win the audience even if he couldn't win the argument. Among his many books and pamphlets, Deedat wrote *Muhammad the Natural Successor to Christ, 50,000 errors in the Bible?, Crucifixion or Cruci-Fiction*[42] and many others that mock and attack the Christian faith. He was a master of his art, making fun of his opponents and playing to his audience till they cheered him on. It really did little to persuade those who were not already convinced.

To attack and undermine is sterile and unhelpful. To examine and question is another thing. Volumes have been written (and can be studied by those with diligence and time) which compare the great religious books of the world's faiths. The study of comparative religion can be a lifetime endeavour – and thank God, some have made it so. We can benefit from their studies.

The heart of the matter

The issue that is central to us here is the truth of the Bible, and with the echoes of a thousand competing claims in our minds, that is surely what we must affirm. If I am sure of my foundations, then I will be in a good position to begin to examine and compare other creeds. If I discover that my foundations are inadequate or faulty, that may be the time to look at the claims of others.

As a Christian, brought up in a Christian home and church, I assumed quite naturally that the Bible is the Word of God, and that God speaks to us through his Word. That is orthodox Christian belief, and it is what the Bible itself affirms:

> In the past God spoke to our forefathers through the prophets at many times and in various ways, but in these last days he has spoken to us by his Son ...[43]

> All Scripture is God-breathed and is useful for teaching, rebuking, correcting and training in righteousness ...[44]

That is the central claim of the Christian Scriptures. God has spoken, and this is the record of his words. This was nevertheless one of the first big mosquitoes to attack me after I became a Christian.

Was the Bible really the authentic voice of God and totally trustworthy? Or was that just an assumption I had inherited from my background? As a product of a fairly narrow Protestant upbringing, in my circle the truth of the Bible was taken for granted. But how could I be sure that it was a valid universal claim, binding not only for me but also for the rest of the world? If truth is absolute, that question needed a good answer. Was the Bible really the Word of God? It was absolutely vital to be sure.

These are doubts that reach us through our intellect, and the questions they raise need serious and detailed intellectual answers. It is a study that takes the commitment of a lifetime, and this small book is not the place for anything but the briefest introduction. Let me nevertheless outline the reasoning that I have found most convincing and helpful. (Some useful books are mentioned in the 'Further Reading' section at the end of the book.) Here now are just three reasons, briefly introduced, that have helped me to cling, sometimes precariously, to the belief that the Bible can be trusted as the Word and words of God.

1. Jesus accepted it and he can be trusted

This may sound like a circular argument, but it contains profound logic. There are reasons outside of Scripture why I am able to find Jesus trustworthy, reasons that are related to his life and teaching and how they have impacted my experience. They have to do with the imprint of divine authenticity on his character and his resurrection from the dead. Because I trust him and believe him to be both unique and infallible (a view shared by many even from other religions or none), I am inclined to trust his view of Scripture. J. I. Packer said in one of his helpful little volumes that it is a mistake 'to ignore the fact that Jesus and his apostles taught a definite doctrine of the nature of Scripture, a doctrine just as integral to their message as were their beliefs about the character of God'.[45] Jesus taught that 'the Scripture cannot be broken'[46] and his confidence in its truth is much easier to accept than the doubts of his critics. This overrides many other difficulties I face in the Scriptures, but of course it is an answer that can relate only to the Old Testament – Jesus' Bible.

2. Jesus communicated that confident trustworthiness to the apostles

The authority of Jesus Christ stretches back to his roots in Old Testament revelation and also forward to the message passed on through the apostles to the church. Jesus gave a promise to his disciples, especially in relation to the assurance of his continued presence through the Holy Spirit: 'He will guide you into all the truth.'[47] That is a small assurance but, buttressed by further claims, amounts to phenomenal authority for the small group of apostles who preserved the truth of the message, and communicated it in writing, after Jesus had physically departed.

3. The personal conviction of the New Testament writers

Personal conviction is no proof of truth or authenticity and many other convinced people have been sincerely deluded. But the apostles were a group of men who were not only willing to die for their convictions, but they had the authority of extraordinary experience. Their credibility derived from their commitment to integrity of the highest order. 'Even if we or an angel from heaven should preach a gospel other than the one we preached to you, let him be condemned!'[48] Strong words from the apostle Paul, but they were recognized as valid by the other apostles and have been accepted as words of truth and authority by the church for centuries since.

Don't just take my word for it. There is a lifetime of fascinating and complex study in this subject, but it is the most important truth to be sure of if we are to survive as credible followers of Christ in this cynical and complicated age. A host of questions remain still unanswered in my mind, but in principle I know that good answers can be found if I look in the right places, and the Bible can be trusted.

Signposts on the way

The truth of the Bible is such an important issue that intellectual enquiry alone is not going to satisfy. There must be much wider reasons why, among so many conflicting voices, I still claim to be a Christian with some integrity. So before we move on to other things, let me give a few of the thoughts which have helped me and enabled me to continue to believe and live as a Christian. These are not strong proofs for the truth of the Bible. But, aligned with the convictions of my mind, they affirm the truth of what I believe and confirm that the path of Christian discipleship makes sense both in mind and in experience.

Let the sun shine

I was travelling on a train through Pakistan and struck up conversation with a Muslim student. At such times it is not always safe or wise to begin to compare religions, so I was avoiding comparisons between our faiths. But he was not so cautious, and he made a comment that I have never forgotten: 'When the sun is shining, you have no need of a light-bulb.' Of course he meant it in the opposite way in which I have looked on it ever since. He wanted me to know that in the light of the glory of God's final revelation in Islam, there is no further need for outmoded religions like Christianity.

I understood something quite different. In the light of the glory of Christ – his message of grace, forgiveness and the promise of life – all other faiths pale. Who wishes to return to the regime of law and condemnation when Jesus has died to give us freedom from guilt and judgment? It is the message of the book of Hebrews. Jewish believers under pressure were being constrained to return to legalism and ritual. 'Therefore ... fix your thoughts on Jesus, the apostle and high priest whom we confess.' It would take more than a lifetime to examine every flower in the garden, but when you have found a perfect flower that fulfils every dream, give yourself to it and enjoy its fragrance.

God has spoken

The Bible itself teaches that there are other ways in which God has revealed himself. The Bible is not the only way.

God has made himself known through the splendour of nature. At least he has made known his 'invisible qualities – his eternal power and divine nature'[49] through his natural creation.

God has also expressed himself in every person's conscience in some way. Even those who have no other knowledge of the God of the Bible show that 'the requirements of the law are written on their hearts, their conscience also bearing witness'.[50]

There is further evidence (though sometimes this is more controversial among Christians) that God has revealed himself in other ways apart from the narrow confines of the Book. The pagans in Athens worshipped an 'unknown God' whom the apostle Paul did not condemn as an idol. On the contrary, he implied that this God was 'not far from each one of us'. Even their own heathen poets were aware that they were his offspring.[51]

There is evidence that God made himself known to, and through, pagan peoples all through history. Think of the way in which Nebuchadnezzar came to know God in the book of Daniel through the 'miraculous signs and wonders that the Most High God has performed for me'.[52] Think too of the heathen tyrant Cyrus, whom God called 'his anointed, Cyrus whose right hand I take hold of'.[53]

I do not wish to deny that God may have revealed himself in incomplete but definite terms to and through people of many different faiths (or no faith) who have set out to seek him with all their hearts. Surely some shadows of his truth are reflected in many of the great religious books of the world. Let us not limit what God might have done, or how he may have made himself known, even while we affirm that his supreme and sufficient revelation is through Christ as recorded in the Bible.

Word alive

I was given my first Bible as a christening present when I was a few weeks old. I didn't even look inside it. I was more interested in sucking my thumb. At school we used to attend morning prayers every day, and I won a prize for reading 2 Samuel 18 aloud. I went through a religious phase around the time I was confirmed in the Church of England and read Bible Reading Fellowship notes every day for a few weeks, but found them boring and irrelevant. It didn't last long.

We had religious lessons in school, and I tried my best to learn something. But it was all a meaningless and irrelevant blur. Two years at university made no difference even though I continued to go to church occasionally. My room-mate sat me down one Sunday evening and said, 'Let's study the Bible.' Out of a sense of duty I obliged and we read through the first chapter of John's Gospel. It was a mass of meaningless words to me. 'In the beginning was the Word' made no sense.

And then I surrendered my life to Christ. I told him that, whatever he wanted, I was ready for. I opened the Bible once more. Incredibly, it made sense. To this day it still amazes me that something that had been so complicated and meaningless one day should become so alive, relevant and readable the next.

I read and read, happily skipping over things that I didn't understand and finding meaning everywhere. It was evidence of the reality of the verse that says: 'No-one knows the thoughts of God except the Spirit of God. We have not received the spirit of the world but the Spirit who is from God, that we may understand . . . '[54] I was so excited that I told everyone what now seemed so clear, and was amazed that others still remained so indifferent.

It is an experience that many others have had, that once the Spirit of Christ comes into a person, he gives understanding of the mysteries of the Bible. In the same way, Jesus 'opened their minds so they could understand the Scriptures' after his resurrection.[55] It is a miracle and it speaks louder than many arguments to those who have experienced it.

The witness of history

A large proportion of the Bible is a record of historical events. Its theology is rooted in, and related to, real space-time happenings – not imaginary or idealized history, but down-to-earth, warts-and-all history.

For this reason the Old Testament is full of genealogies. Who has not got bogged down in their Bible reading with the endless lists of names of ancestors long forgotten? I struggle every time my regular Bible reading brings me to 1 Chronicles. For nine long chapters we plough through lists of obscure names – 'all

Israel was listed in the genealogies'.[56] Whatever is the relevance of that for twenty-first-century Christians?

Its relevance is that it roots God's revelation in the lives of real people. Both Judaism and Christianity regularly celebrate historical events. The Passover festival, which is still the annual highlight of the Jewish religious year, is a celebration of events that took place more than 4,000 years ago. When we break bread and drink wine together we are celebrating a historical event whose consequences are with us today.

Contrast, if you will, the philosophical and religious sayings of the Buddha, the mythology of Hinduism, the wise sayings of Confucius or even the religious teachings of the Quran and Islamic tradition. None of them depends for its veracity on the witness of history or the claim to be founded on empirical evidence.

The imprint of truth

In 1967 J. B. Phillips, the Bible translator, wrote a little book called *The Ring of Truth*. It is a translator's testimony to the evidence that convinced him that the book he was translating was no ordinary book, but the very Word of God with power to change lives. He gave his reasons for writing the book in his foreword:

> For twenty-five years I have written for the ordinary man who is no theologian. Alas, today, he frequently gets the impression that the New Testament is no longer historically reliable.
>
> What triggered off my anger against some of our 'experts' is this. A clergyman, old, retired, useless if you like, took his own life because his reading of the 'new theology' and even some programmes on television, finally drove him, in his loneliness and ill-health, to conclude that his own life's work had been founded upon a lie ...
>
> I say quite bluntly that some of the intellectuals ... who write so cleverly and devastatingly about the Christian

faith appear to have no personal knowledge of the living God.[57]

Television is a medium that is always looking for something new and controversial, because controversy attracts viewers. In this field originality is more important than truth. Channel 4 TV aired a programme in which a panel of 'experts' set out to 'prove' that our New Testament books are a collection of theological theories written under the influence of the apostle Paul. What we have, therefore, in our Bibles, they said, exuding authority, is not a picture of the real Jesus, but a fabrication by Paul, a clever and ingenious schemer. Channel 4's experts then set out to reconstruct what the 'true' gospel would have said if it had ever been written, and what the 'real' Jesus would have been like.

It was a work of sensational speculation and imagination, designed to undermine traditional belief and do exactly what made J. B. Phillips so angry. He ended his little book with these words:

> It is my serious conclusion that we have here in the New Testament words that bear the hall-mark of reality and the ring of truth.

The proof of the pudding

It seems to me that a very convincing way to define the nature of the truth is to look at its results. 'By their fruit you will recognize them,' said Jesus, referring of course to false prophets, though the principle is valid in a wider context. 'A good tree cannot bear bad fruit, and a bad tree cannot bear good fruit.'[58]

Some years ago I watched a television programme about the extraordinary life of a convicted killer who had spent many years in prison. The programme investigated his claim to have been transformed through faith in Christ. David Lant had been a particularly vicious and unpleasant character, his life eaten up by hatred and bitterness. He and another inmate had brutally murdered another prisoner, for which he received a life sentence. The *Daily Telegraph* (24 February 2000) described him as 'the Broadmoor torturer ... an inmate who took part in one of the country's most sadistic and violent prison sieges'.

In 1986 David became a Christian. 'You could have knocked me down with a feather,' he wrote. 'I knew that the Lord Jesus had spoken to me ... I had received a pardon for every single one of my horrendous sins because I had truly believed in him.' The change in his life was so remarkable that the BBC made a documentary about him. He had started a ministry from his prison cell, translating Christian books in many languages into Braille for the blind.

The documentary focused on the old question: Is his conversion genuine? Will it last? They interviewed the prison psychiatrist, whose 'professional' convictions could not accept that such conversions were ever genuine or would last. But David radiated genuine transformation. I wrote to the BBC and ultimately corresponded for a short while with David. He is still in prison, still serving the Lord and helping the blind world-wide. He says:

> He has taught me so much since I became his disciple. I think the most important thing to me is that without Jesus I am number 467638, a prisoner of this world; but with Jesus I am an adopted son of God ...

Is the Bible true, the unique Word of God? I believe so, and the proof of the pudding is in the eating.

Living with questions

Those mosquitoes still bother me – many questions remain. The exclusive claims of the Bible do not stand alone. They must be seen in the light of the personal status and claims of Jesus Christ. I have come to know and trust in Christ, and for forty years I have not found fault with him either in his Word or in my experience of him. That alone overrules many a thorny problem.

But that cannot be our last word on the complex issues of the Bible. In the next chapter we take a closer look at the Book itself. Suppose that it really is God's final Word to humanity – which is what we Christians maintain and, with difficulty, I believe. Does it have the ring of truth and the clarity of message that one would expect from such a book? If God has spoken, has he spoken in the clear and convincing terms that such a message surely deserves?

6

Making Sense of the Book
How can it possibly be true?

I had only been in India for a few weeks before I was made leader of an evangelism team. Needless to say, I was ill-equipped and unprepared, but we survived somehow. I always considered that if you have a good team, the chances are they will think you are a good leader. So it was with us. I thought they were wonderful and we got on well together.

As part of the team schedule we had a study hour, when someone would lead a Bible study. I decided that I would take a series on the Bible. It seemed important to me to have good reasons for believing that the Bible is the Word of God, especially when faced every day with Hindus and Muslims who believe otherwise.

I pulled out some notes and started to examine the Bible. To set the tone, we began by asking some hard questions, such as:

- *Why is the Bible any more special than any other book?*
- *What grounds do we have to think that the Bible is inspired and a book by Billy Graham is not?*
- *Who put the Bible together? And why should we suppose they did a good job?*
- *What about the supposed contradictions in the Bible? How can they be reconciled?*
- *What about all those genealogies? Are they as inspired as the Gospels?*

- *Why is the Old Testament so full of bloodthirsty passages? Are they compatible with the message of God's love?*
- *Is the whole Book a cultural relic? Or is it relevant for us today?*

All of these are questions that have caused problems for me and demanded answers, and I could extend the list. Ever since I started reading the Bible after I gave my life to Christ, I have received endless inspiration and help from it, but not without a struggle.

After my initial study was over, one young man from South India came to me in private.

'Why did you raise all those questions?' he asked. 'I don't see any reason for having this study.'

I tried to explain, telling him how important it was that we should have answers to the questions we might get asked about the Bible's inspiration and authority.

He was lost for words. 'I don't understand,' he said. 'The Bible is *the Bible*. That's enough for me. I think it is wrong to raise questions about it.'

How wonderful to have such a simple trust in God's Word! If it is so simple for you too, perhaps you should skip this chapter – maybe throw the whole book away – because my small mind still asks searching questions about the special place we give to the Bible, and some of the strange ways in which it tells us the truth.

Shortly after I arrived in India, we had a visit from a great and respected Bible teacher, William MacDonald. He came to spend Christmas with us in Calcutta. I had read one or two of his books. In fact one of them, *True Discipleship*, was required reading for everyone who joined OM in those days, and for that reason we stood in awe of him.

I remember asking him only one question. 'Have you ever had any doubts about the Bible? Do you ever question whether it is really the Word of God?'

His answer ran something like this: 'Since the day I gave my life to Christ, I can honestly say I have never for one moment had any doubts about the truth of the Bible.'

He silenced me, and my amazement at him grew. Was it possible that anyone could live in such conviction? Was he naïve? Did he never think through the issues or battle with the complexities? Or was there something badly wrong with me that made me struggle so much?

I concluded that we were just different. Some people are gifted with the ability to sail through life in wonderful assurance, and others are condemned to battle with hard questions.

Persistent difficulties

Let us look more closely at some of the persistent difficulties that have plagued and stimulated me in the course of my forty years of Bible study. They are the kind of problems that cynics and atheists accuse us of ignoring. They are the reasons why people have rejected the inerrancy of the Scriptures, and why some have overthrown the Christian faith altogether. Due to the confines of this book, this list is far from complete.

- *If God wanted to tell us that we needed to be saved, and then give us a formula by which we could become reconciled to him, why did he make the Bible so complicated? It is not a simple Book. Theologians have worked overtime to make its teachings clearer and more systematic. If God wanted us to understand his plan clearly and systematically, why didn't he give us a book of systematic theology instead?*

- *The Old Testament is full of crude and bloody stories that have little relevance to modern living or any standards of decency and civilization. Consider the ugly tale of the slaughter of 3,000 men by the Levites after the destruction of the golden calf,[59] or the prophet Samuel who 'hewed Agag in pieces before the Lord in Gilgal'.[60] Why is there so much violence throughout the Bible?*

- *Was all that blood in the desert necessary? Or is it just a hangover from a primitive pagan attempt to appease a supposedly angry deity?*

- *God's wrath burns throughout the pages of the Old Testament. God seems to have been angry even at small details that wouldn't even land us in court. He sent a plague on Israel which killed 70,000 men, because David took a census of the people.[61] And he killed Uzzah as they were bringing the ark of the covenant back to Jerusalem, because he 'reached out his hand to steady the ark, because the oxen stumbled'.[62]*

- *The status of women in the Bible is highly questionable, especially in the Old Testament. Admittedly, there are some outstanding exceptions, but on the whole the Bible appears to present, and approve of, a strongly patriarchal society, in which women clearly take second place. Add to this the vulgar insult of polygamy and the multitudes of concubines that some of God's chosen kings took to themselves, and still won his favour.*

A digression

In order to approach some answers to these problems, I want to digress a little. We will re-join the main road once we have made a little excursion down a side-track.

I think it is important and helpful to realize that there are really no unbelievers in the world. Everyone believes in something, even if it is only Marxist dialectics or the omnipotence of science. Everyone is a theologian of some kind!

What do I mean by that? Theology is by definition the understanding of God, his existence, his nature, his characteristics, his actions. Everyone has some sort of belief about God, even if it is a belief in his non-existence. However, most people (as we have seen from opinion polls) actually do have some beliefs about God and they are invariably derived from some source.

Inherited beliefs

Many people accept the ideas about God they have received from their upbringing, whether it is from their parents, or through church attendance, or by instruction from the *mullah* or the Hindu priest. This has come to be accepted as the norm. Those born in Roman Catholic homes will normally adopt Catholic theology. Those born in a Protestant home will be Protestant in their theology. Those born to Muslim parents will be believers in Islam, and so on. Such beliefs form part of most people's cultural comfort zone.

Invented beliefs

Very commonly people decide at some stage in life to break free (as far as they understand freedom) from their traditions and invent a god of their own imagination, probably somewhat different from the image they have inherited. The new creation is often a mixture of the nice elements of traditional religion (such as, God is love) and something to help them feel good (God wants to make us happy, helps us pass exams and makes us comfortable about ourselves).

Cocktail beliefs

Many people choose a cocktail of creeds to suit their mood. The singer Boy George, who was brought up by 'mildly devout Irish Roman Catholic parents', now says: 'I'll have, like, six months meditating every day, then I'll stop and do yoga ... when I lived in squats I had chintzy statues of Jesus hanging round ... In the hall, we had a picture of the Pope hanging next to a picture of Muhammad Ali. I feel that that was a healthy balance.'[63] In other words, he has devised a pot-pourri of acceptable tastes to suit his image.

Consumer beliefs

The BBC TV series *The Soul of Britain* gave some fascinating insights into the 'average' approach to religion in twenty-first-century Britain. Linda Woodhead, a sociologist from the University of Lancaster, had this to say:

> Whereas once a lot of religion ... was packaged and regulated, you would go to church at a certain time and an authoritarian teaching would be given you, it has become now much more a matter of choice, and you find people personalizing religion – taking bits that fit with what they want in a particular stage of their life and putting together some sort of package that they feel makes sense for them.[64]

Professor Steve Bruce added a further insight:

> They act as consumers. They put together their own particular packages from what is now a completely global cafeteria of spiritual ideas.

Adopted beliefs

Many Christians obtain their theology from books they read, sermons they listen to or the ethos of the church fellowship they attend. I think of the huge influence of the fantasy novels of Frank Peretti or the popular writings of Benny Hinn. Others formulate their theology from popular worship songs. Happily, many hymns and worship songs have strong biblical foundations, but it has to be said that others are closer to current fads in the Christian world than to the Bible.

Second-hand beliefs

Many Christians build their theology around a particular teacher or charismatic (in the broad sense of the term) leader. This is as true in the non-Christian world, with leaders like Sai Baba in India and Ayatolla Khomeni in Iran, as it is in the Christian world. The devotion inspired by men like Dr Martyn

Lloyd-Jones or Watchman Nee has had both good and bad effects, but their forceful leadership style has inspired generations of devotees.

The truth in all of this is that everyone has a theology – a set of personal beliefs about the Deity. And all of those beliefs have been obtained from some strong influence in their lives. That is true even of those (perhaps especially of those) who have invented their own version of God.

Why do I say all this?

Because it justifies to me, very forcibly, the value of the Bible, and especially the Old Testament, and it overrules many of the problems and objections I have struggled with as outlined above.

Many people's objections to the Old Testament are based on an assessment of how they believe it ought to have been. As though to say, 'I don't like the way God led the people out of Egypt. They should have gone by a different route.' Or, 'I don't appreciate the instructions God gave for the treatment of leprosy. He should have inspired people with modern principles of hygiene.' Or, 'I would prefer a God who didn't get angry so easily.'

So where are we going to go to find the truth? Are we going to come to the Bible with our cultural preconceptions and pick and choose what suits us? Or are we in a position to trust that God has revealed himself in this Book and therefore we are ready to listen to what he has to say? That is faith – not a blind step into the dark, but a reasoned willingness to listen.

If I do not bend my mind to understand the Bible and persist in seeing its problems, then I have no choice but to go with the flow and look for my theology elsewhere. My mind has good reasons for wanting to understand.

Objections overruled?

If I were God (God forbid!) and understood how people resented and resisted my authority so fervently, I would need to be persistent in making my point. I would need to teach my lessons forcibly, regularly and repeatedly. If I knew that people had their heads filled with preconceptions and wrong ideas about Me – ideas which they had picked up from all sorts of wrong places – how would I act to correct those ideas? If I saw that they had led them into bad practices, idolatrous worship forms, crude attempts to fulfil carnal needs and damaging lifestyles, how would I drum the truth into their very stubborn minds?

Here are some of the truths God had to get people to understand, even though accepting them often did not (and still often does not) come naturally or easily:

God is holy and sometimes very frightening

The God of the Bible is to be feared as well as respected. Only in the light of the cross can such fear be dealt with and God become an intimate Friend and Father. The people of Israel were very slow to learn this lesson and we are very slow to remember it today. We would all much prefer to have a tolerant God (an all-embracing and jolly Father Christmas) who is willing to permit us to do as we please, in the knowledge that he will turn a blind eye and make us feel good about ourselves once we have achieved what we wanted.

The books of the Law, with all their bloody – and to our clinically tuned culture, crude – ritual, are God's very forcible, graphic and culturally totally appropriate way of telling us that he has high standards and we would be well advised to take him seriously.

In the light of that, what we sometimes read as cruelty can be seen as God's kindness to save humanity from a worse fate. His desire to keep ill-equipped people at arm's length is an act of love to help us see the importance of approaching him suitably. If there had been no warnings at Mount Sinai, the people would have been burned to a cinder by their blind folly. Furthermore, we would never have understood God's extraordinary act of generosity and grace at Calvary.

Let us not make the mistake of thinking that the New Testament has replaced the 'cruelty' of the Old Testament deity with a God of love. The cross itself makes no sense without a full appreciation of the holiness (and anger and terror) of God and the inevitability of judgment on sinful humanity.

We humans are very stubborn and our hearts are far more deceitful and selfish than we are ever willing to admit to; furthermore, we are very slow to learn

We deceive ourselves very badly if we think that at heart we are good people, or that in any sense God owes us a living. That very idea, which is extremely popular and common even in churches today, is proof that the Old Testament message is in no way under-stated. The history of the people of Israel and of God's repeated attempts to 'civilize' them with his kindness and his law demonstrates over and over again that we are evil and in need of radical salvation surgery.

Modern literature and cinema drive this lesson home far better than the average Sunday sermon. William Golding's *Lord of the Flies* is not alone in depicting human beings as cruel, crude, selfish and greedy by nature. Watch the *Mad Max* films with their bleak portrayal of humanity's mean and brutal fight for self-preservation, or Kevin Costner's haunting *Waterworld*, to see the animal instincts of desperate people. Browse the internet or thumb through the daily papers or a selection of weekly magazines if you want to see how evil we can be.

We seriously fool ourselves if we think we are naturally good people. We are what the Bible states very clearly – an essentially self-centred race that has fallen very far and is much in need of serious treatment to make us what God originally intended us to be.

If we have not grasped that clear Old Testament analysis of human nature, we will never understand the magnitude of the grace of God or the meaning of the cross of Christ.

The Bible recounts, and gives meaning to, the story of the birth of humanity

Humanity has come a long way and we make far too many judgmental assumptions from our latter-day point of view. In the twenty-first century we arrogantly dare to call ourselves 'modern' and we look with disdain at those who lived in the 'dark ages' of long ago. But every generation that has ever lived has considered itself modern. We dare to consider our culture the epitome of enlightened living. But each generation has viewed its own culture in the same way.

Already, at the dawn of the new century, we look back on the 'olden days' of the 1950s when people had black-and-white television and refrigerators were still a luxury. How quickly we pass judgment on the 'primitive' lifestyles of the past. In fifty years' time people will judge our 'modern' society in the same arrogant light and laugh over our naïve fascination with cyber-space and our delight at every new electronic toy.

God did not suddenly create humanity equipped with all the 'modern' advances of human discovery – medicine and hygiene, micro-chip technology and the internet, and all the rest. No, he started from the beginning, when there was no time, no civilization, no moral order, and history was at point zero.

The book of Genesis provides one of the first attempts to write a history that included a true sense of time and accurate dates. The Old Testament represents the first attempt to get facts, genealogies and chronologies right. It is a ground-breaking approach to history, and scientific investigation and archaeological discovery continue to demonstrate that it is trustworthy and accurate.

It is folly to judge such foundational documents of the human race by our latter-day standards or through 'modern' cultural spectacles. Many of our problems with the Old Testament spring from such faulty perspectives.

It is a mistake to pass judgment on the values of the past by the light of present-day standards

A huge shift has taken place in cultural values since the days of the Old Testament, and still we attempt to judge the past by the light of the present. Having lived for many years in Pakistan, which is essentially a very traditional culture, I have learned not to pass judgment so quickly on things I do not at first understand. Things may be different, but only an arrogant person will call them bad for that reason.

Many of our Western values are relatively recent innovations. Take the concept of time and efficiency. Wrist-watches to rule the day have only been in common use since the nineteenth century, yet we judge people today on the basis of promptitude and efficiency – both fairly new cultural innovations.

Old Testament culture values community and family far more highly than individual rights, honour and prestige far more greatly than progress and efficiency. Our society, which puts such high value on personal freedom, quality of life and human rights, is all too quick to find fault with the message of the Scriptures because it does not emphasize what we consider to be of importance.

The Bible as a harmony presents us with solutions and answers to great world questions that hang together to form a unified whole in a way that no other world-view can offer

While the world (with its closed-system world-view) looks for answers to the origins and the composition of society and human nature, the Bible offers a reasonable explanation. While people struggle to make sense of suffering and human greed, and to understand the resentments that mar race relations, the Bible offers an explanation. While society grapples with issues of its own identity, the Bible sets forth a pattern that has been tried for centuries and found to work.

Here is a unified world-view that begins with the beginning, explains the origins of evil and the relationship between humans and the animal and vegetable kingdoms, proposes an ideal pattern of relationship between the sexes and races, and holds out hope for the future with rational explanations. The Bible proposes logical answers to many of the world's greatest questions, if only we are humble enough to recognize and accept them.

People without God and his revelation have rejected these principles and have forgotten how to swim. No wonder Schaeffer said that 'modern man has his feet firmly planted in mid-air'. The Bible, warts and all, gives a firm and solid foundation on which to stand.

The Bible is a marvellous statement of human experience, with the stamp of divine accuracy

One of the extraordinary things about the Bible is its humanness. There is no cover-up, no pretence that great men and women of God were anything but fallible and weak creatures of flesh and blood. The Bible is not a book of super-heroes with whom we cannot identify.

With the same degree of mystery that Jesus the Son of God was also totally human, so the Bible is the Word of God and yet a totally human record. That does not mean it contains mistakes and errors, any more than Jesus' humanity indicated that he was a sinner. The Bible purports to present us with God's perspective on the world and God's purpose for mankind. But because it is a human record, it contains human emotion, the admissions of human failure and many human cries for help.

That means the Bible is a mystery, but it also gives it its endless appeal. It speaks to us with authority, and brings us a word of comfort. We can identify with its emotions, because they are so like our own experiences of need.

Just imagine . . .

To appreciate what the Bible is, with all of its mysteries and complexities, just consider how our world would be different if we had no Bible – no Ten Commandments, no insight into the biblical origins of human history, no teaching on sin or salvation, no understanding of righteousness or law, no Christ and no gospel. If there were no evidence that there is a God in eternity who cares for his creation, the prospect for humanity would be bleak.

So much of what we today term 'civilization' owes its origins to the Bible that it is impossible to conceive a world without it. The very thought is depressing to contemplate. Space prevents us from expanding on the nightmare.

7

Why Jesus?
Peering into the fog

I had a friend called Tom who claimed that he came to know
God in three stages. 'First,' he said, 'I came to know God the
Father, the spiritual power that pervades the universe. Then
some time later I came to know Jesus as my personal Saviour. A
long time afterwards I came to know the Holy Spirit and his
power in my life. They were three distinct encounters.'

I never understood Tom or his experiences, nor did I accept
his testimony as either orthodox or biblical, and certainly it is
not to be recommended to others. At the same time, I could not
refute Tom's experience (however much I might question his
explanations), and so accepted that his experience was just
'different'. After all, no two people have exactly the same
experience, and even the New Testament makes it clear that
there are a variety of ways in which people come to know
God.

But it raises some intriguing questions.

God, by definition, is surely beyond our full understanding.
No finite mind can ever comprehend infinity, nor can the
physical adequately understand the spiritual. Germaine Greer
speaks of God as 'this unimaginable idea'[65] and she is not alone
in being bewildered by the concept. The available views
concerning the nature of God are innumerable. Probably the
most common 'street view' of God today has more in common
with the Hindu concept of 'Om' or Brahma – the ground of

all being, the spirit in nature, the eternal incomprehensible. New-Agers have taken to extravagant extremes what many people believe in practice – that God is a nice idea that we can use to make ourselves comfortable, an undefined fog vaguely related to the stars, the trees and mother earth, to be manipulated for human convenience. I can find some sympathy for those who exercise their creative imagination to guess what God must be like.

The Old Testament in some respects shares similar views on the mystery of the eternal, though conceding that the 'undefined fog' actually has personality and a mind that has graciously given us humans a more detailed picture of himself through various means of self-disclosure. But still there remain huge areas that are undefined and unclear.

- Abraham is called the 'friend of God' but in all his encounters with him there is an aura of intriguing mystery. Think of the strange visit of Melchizedek who brought out bread and wine and blessed him.[66] Was he a divine figure? Think of the 'thick and dreadful darkness' that fell on Abraham when God made a covenant with him.[67] Or the three messengers that appeared to him at the oaks of Mamre, with whom he interceded for Sodom.[68] He is the one whom Jacob describes as 'the God of Abraham and the Fear of Isaac'.[69] Every encounter conceals as much as it reveals.

- God the mysterious is a Being of extraordinary complexity. He 'lives in unapproachable light'[70] and 'in him there is no darkness at all'.[71] And yet when Moses climbed Mount Sinai to meet him, he 'approached the thick darkness where God was'.[72] Is he a Being of essential contradiction? Did the Bible writers make a mistake? Or is God just hard to describe and hard to comprehend?

- To Moses God said: 'I will cause all my goodness to pass in front of you, and I will proclaim my name, the Lord ... But you cannot see my face; for no-one may see me and live.'[73] And yet the prophet Ezekiel saw 'the appearance of the likeness of the glory of the Lord'[74] seated before him upon a throne. So indescribable and so dazzling was the image he saw that he could not find the words to explain his vision, except in vague terms of light and value.

- Isaiah saw the Lord, but his face and feet were hidden, and the prophet was terrified. He made no attempt to describe the appearance of God. The whole vision filled him with fear, the foundations of the building shook and the house was filled with smoke.[75] Yet a few verses earlier he had the cheek to say that God 'whistles for those at the end of the earth'.[76] Is he describing the same deity?

God, by definition, is hidden from view, too high and holy to look at, too extraordinary to comprehend. Even the apostle Paul said of him that he 'alone is immortal and ... lives in unapproachable light, whom no-one has seen or can see'.[77]

In common, I believe, with many, I have passed through turmoil trying to grapple with an adequate understanding of the nature of God. Who is this infinite, invisible Being who expects us to believe the incredible about himself? I can't see him. I can't feel him. He is out of reach of the exploration of my senses.

In popular theology – the kind of belief system that makes few intellectual demands and carries most people along on a wave of good feelings – there is little serious effort to understand the nature of God. Some attempts are made to picture him in cuddly terms, as a cosmic Daddy who is ready to give us a hug when we feel lonely, or 'the Man upstairs' of popular humour. Traditional art has imprinted its images on our minds to no better effect. The bearded Creator of Michelangelo's Sistine Chapel does the true image of God no service.

But look up into the sky on a dark, clear night, and think: 'That is God – out there in the distant reaches of space', or attempt to reach out to the invisible nothingness that is all around, and try to picture the One in whom 'we live and move and have our being'.[78] That is the God the pagan Athenians were reaching out for with little success. I feel a close affinity to them at times. The mystery is vast and intangible.

The true God we Christians claim to believe in is the God above and beyond, the unimaginable One who, we say, existed before anything else and whom we simply refer to as 'God'. He (or it) is beyond imagination, holy and, evidently, sometimes dangerous. How can we possibly relate to such a One? By definition of his holiness, he is 'totally other', and we are at a complete loss when we try to relate to him in these terms.

So what does Jesus Christ have to do with all this? As Christians we tritely call him God and so equate him with this totally incomprehensible One we have been trying to explore.

I recall the first time I watched the 1964 film *The Greatest Story Ever Told*, as a student in Dublin. Max von Sydow acts the part of Jesus in a sweeping and imaginative reconstruction of the events, which looks quaintly dated today but was very vivid back in the sixties. Von Sydow is tall, handsome and impressive, but there is one particular scene that haunted me.

It is in Bethany and Lazarus has just died. His body has been put into the tomb and then they send for Jesus. As we watch, he comes striding across the hillside towards the waiting women. 'Lord,' says Martha, 'if you had been here, my brother would not have died.'

'Your brother will rise again,' replies Jesus.

'I know he will rise again in the resurrection at the last day.' She gives an orthodox Jewish answer based on a traditional hope.

And then come the stunning words, as recorded in the Gospel of John: 'I am the resurrection and the life. He who believes in me will live, even though he dies; and whoever lives and believes in me will never die. Do you believe this?'[79]

Hang on a moment, I thought. This guy may be tall and impressive, but to all intents and purposes he is an ordinary man, and here he is telling us that if we believe in him we will never die. If it was just Max von Sydow — or even the Pope or Billy Graham — I would think him crazy to make such a claim.

Who is this Jesus, that he can say such a thing and get away with it? Anyone else would be ignored, treated as a joke or considered mad.

But he went on not only to bring Lazarus back to life, but to attract millions to believe that he is God. That is extraordinary. If that man is truly God, then what does that tell me about who God is?

The very incomprehensible mystery of God makes an explanation necessary if we are to relate to him in any way. Could this man Jesus really be the key that unlocks the dark secret, the mould that forms the fog into a shape we can understand?

Eternal mystery in human terms

I have found it helpful to look at it in this way. Picture a great city that you have never visited. The city is surrounded by high walls and it is impossible to look over them. You exist in the desert that surrounds the city walls. As the Bible pictures it, we have chosen to live outside the city. Our ancestors made the stupid choice and opted for independence in the desert rather than obedience in the city, and that has landed us in this wasteland.

In some respects we do quite well in the desert. We have discovered all kinds of things about living with sand. We have discovered how to exploit it, use it for our own ends, build homes in it and amuse ourselves making sand-castles. A lot of people have decided that the city is just a myth, and that we can live very well without it, though that is not the normal reaction of the majority. Many realize that there must be more to life – after all, the desert sand must have come from somewhere – and maybe a greater Reality does exist. Possibly there really is a city that hides these secrets within its walls. People are curious, for a variety of reasons, to know more about it.

Not surprisingly, many people just sit in the sand and make wild guesses about the city and the secrets that lie behind its high walls. Some of the guesses are almost inspired, considering the evidence that is available. Many surmise, for example, that God-inside-the-city must bear some similarity to people-in-the-desert. It is a good guess, considering that he originated us.

Others assume that since we have some moral conscience, God-inside-the-city probably has some moral values also. Since the sun shines on the city as well as the desert, that too tells us something about the nature of life inside the great walls.

The great adventure – certainly the greatest adventure humanity has ever attempted – is not just to guess what is inside the city, but actually to get inside those walls. That is the great quest of all religion, and it has led to much confusion throughout history. So-called 'prophets' have come and gone, some making a greater impression than others, some building up vast empires and hordes of followers who have been inspired by their theories. Some of them have pretended to have special insight into the city's mysteries. Some have even attempted to scale the walls or dig beneath their foundations.

And then, remarkably, one day out of the mist Someone appears who says that he has been inside the city. In fact he says words to this effect: 'No-one has gone into the city except the one who came out from the city – that is I, a special representative of the human race (the Son of man).'[80]

So what? Many fools make outrageous claims. Anyone can wander in from the desert and claim to have come from God. In fact throughout history hundreds have set themselves up as prophets, gurus and teachers. What is different about this one?

It is indeed an extraordinary claim and, of course, we should only take it seriously after we have made careful examination of his credentials, found out about his history and his origins, examined his behaviour and teaching, and discovered whether anything makes him different enough to make his claim remotely credible.

To those who stay around to listen, he goes on: 'I am going back inside that city to prepare a place for you. And if I go and get a place ready for you inside the city, I will come back and take you to be with Me there.' His followers are incredulous. One of them says, 'That's ridiculous. We don't know the way.'[81]

'Don't worry,' he says. 'I am the Way.'[82]

He says a lot of other, similar things, all equally outrageous. Among other boasts he says that, in fulfilment of the dreams and hopes of all those who have been hunting for a way into the city, now at last there is a doorway. He says, 'I am the doorway.'[83]

Is it any wonder that some people think he is not only mad but also dangerous? The more he says and does, the more extreme and amazing it becomes. The consequences of his claims become threatening to the establishment and disturbing to the *status quo*. But his disciples – those who know him the most intimately and live closest to him – are increasingly persuaded. They see something in this person that causes the clouds to lift and the fog to part. He has the ring of truth.

I have lived close to a number of extraordinary people over the years, people who have hit the spotlight in one way or another and made an impact on their world. But to be honest, the closer I have come to outstanding people, the more I have seen their faults and their ordinariness. It is disappointing. Our heroes always crash when we come too close to them. As a general rule, it is wise to keep our heroes at a distance, because we are bound to be disillusioned if we get too close. But not so with Jesus. Those who were the closest to him were the most convinced.

- *You want to know what God the Father is like – the mystery behind the walls?* Jesus told his disciple Philip: 'He is like Me.' 'Anyone who has seen me has seen the Father.'[84]
- *You thought God was invisible, intangible, incomprehensible?* 'No-one has ever seen God; the only Son ... he has made him known.'[85] Jesus is his image. Look at him. Touch him. Listen to him. He will show you what God is like. 'He is the image of the invisible God.'[86] His intimate followers were convinced of this.
- *All that mystical, ethereal, incomprehensible mystery that we call 'God'?* Now we have cause to believe that this Jesus – this person who walked the Galilean hills two thousand years ago – is God. 'God was pleased to have all his fullness dwell in him.'[87]

Do you see what has suddenly happened? It is as though all the fury and mystery of that invisible eternity has become focused into the person of Jesus Christ, just as the light of the sun becomes concentrated into a pinpoint by a powerful magnifying glass.

At this point it is very tempting to say, 'That's impossible. No human being could become concentrated deity. It makes no rational sense.' God is God – by definition eternal, vast, distant, intangible, the One who lives among the stars. Jesus was a man – he brushed his teeth, spat and combed his hair like any other human being. How can you dare to equate him with the Creator God?

But it is important to take a long, hard look at Jesus rather than reject his outrageous claims, for several reasons:

Intimate acquaintance

These are not claims about Jesus invented by hermits who never knew him or by theologians out of touch with reality. They are the convictions of people who knew him intimately. Some people accuse the apostle Paul of inventing a lot of the theology of the New Testament, but most of the strongest claims do not come from Paul. They come from Jesus' most intimate friend John, the 'disciple whom Jesus loved',[88] who is reliably assumed to have written the Gospel that bears his name.

That is not proof in itself. As one cynic pointed out to me, Hitler's secretary died still convinced that he was a great patriot, betrayed by an uncomprehending world. It is true that Hitler successfully mesmerized an inner circle, which remained convinced to the end that he was someone extraordinary. But that circle was very far from united in their adulation, and millions came to a very different conclusion about him. But Jesus has fascinated believers and unbelievers alike for centuries, and few have ever dared to call him a lunatic, an egomaniac or a cunning deceiver.

For example, John Stuart Mill, a nineteenth-century liberal

philosopher and economist, was no friend of Christianity, and yet he was fascinated by Jesus. He wrote:

> About the life and sayings of Jesus there is a stamp of personal originality combined with profundity of insight in the very first rank of men of sublime genius of whom our species can boast ... The ideal representative and guide of humanity.[89]

Napoleon Bonaparte, intelligent and arrogant as he was, was similarly impressed with Jesus:

> I know men; and I tell you that Jesus Christ is not a man ... There is between Christianity and whatever other religions the distance of infinity. Everything in Christ astonishes me ...[90]

This man, hard as it may be to assimilate, was different and he still impresses humanity with his lifestyle and his words. What can we make of that?

Unreasonable but authentic?

It seems absurd to accept the claim that an apparently illegitimate child, born in a squalid corner of the Roman Empire, was God. In that light it is a claim to be laughed out of court, in spite of the Christmas-card imagery that now surrounds the event. Even when we take into account the authentic supernatural events that accompanied his birth – the prophecies, the angelic appearances, the star – it still takes a huge stretch of the imagination to believe that the God who is responsible for the vast reaches of space, the galaxies and beyond, could be 'contracted to a span' – in other words, born as a human infant to a human mother.

It is no surprise that some Christians in the early church also struggled with this and attempted to embellish the birth with magic to give it a more authentic supernatural ring. A second-century Gnostic writing related that 'Jesus spake even when he was in the cradle, and said to his mother: Mary, I am Jesus the

Son of God ...'[91] and claimed that his swaddling cloth would not burn when thrown into the fire.[92] Another early so-called 'gospel' claimed that the child Jesus fashioned clay birds, clapped his hands and caused them to fly away. These 'miracles' were invented to justify the claim that this child was divine, but they do not bear the mark of authenticity and were rightly rejected.

Likewise, it is no surprise that Islam cannot accept the divinity of Christ, and follows the far more reasonable belief that he was a human prophet – among the greatest, above sin and suffering, but still only a human being. The Jehovah's Witnesses have struggled with the same apparent impossibility and declare Jesus to be a human, separated from deity by infinity.

Yet the Bible affirms that this human being, Jesus, is divine, and that he alone has bridged the infinite gap between the mortal and the immortal, the temporal and the eternal.

- Jesus calmed the storm on the Sea of Galilee, and the disciples were amazed. 'What kind of man is this? Even the winds and the waves obey him!'[93]
- The Jews, angry that a well-known cripple had been healed on the Sabbath day, began to plot Jesus' death because 'not only was he breaking the Sabbath, but he was even calling God his own Father, making himself equal with God'.[94] They could not accept the evidence of their eyes.
- The Jews found it incredible that the one who said 'I am the bread which came down from heaven' was the same person they knew as a carpenter's son in Nazareth, 'the son of Joseph, whose father and mother we know'.[95]
- 'Are you greater than our father Abraham, who died?' they said. 'Who do you claim to be?' The Jews could not stomach the implications of the outrageous claim that this Jesus was greater than their greatest prophet. When Jesus answered, 'Before Abraham was, I am,'[96] they took up stones to kill him.

And for that claim they finally put him to death – a death that has never been forgotten and is still celebrated by millions around the world. Why?

The ultimate proof

The whole extraordinary life of Jesus would be no more than that – an extraordinary life – if the final act had never been realized. By the time he was killed his disciples already were beginning to understand that he was no ordinary human. However amazing were the hints he had given about his nature, his origin and his destiny – not to mention the impeccable way in which he behaved and the miracles which were integral to his lifestyle – his execution by the Roman authorities was devastating to the disciples. There would have been no Christian faith if the next chapter had not been written.

His death was not the end of his story. Three days after his corpse was laid and sealed in a tomb in the rock, he returned convincingly back to life. Volumes have been written on the evidences for the resurrection. The apostle Paul launched its first defence, because his life depended on it:

> If Christ has not been raised, our preaching is useless and so is your faith ... If Christ has not been raised, your faith is futile; you are still in your sins ... But Christ has indeed been raised from the dead ...[97]

For Paul this was no myth, no theological fantasy, no stretch of the imagination. It really happened. For the disciples and for more than 500 others[98] Jesus had mastered death and returned to life. It opened a new chapter for the human race, and provided the cornerstone for a new faith.

The evidences for the physical resurrection of Jesus Christ are numerous and well documented by others, whose books can be read and studied.[99] If the only evidence was the pious hope of the faithful few, it might be possible to dispel it as the superstition of a primitive age. But consider also the records of history. It would be a psychological impossibility to imagine that the resurrection was a delusion, invention or clever fraud. From the first century, many thousands of Jesus' followers have been willing to give their lives for the conviction that their Leader overcame death and returned to life. None of the early disciples ever cracked under interrogation to admit that it was a concocted hoax or an invention of their fertile imaginations. No reasonable alternative explanation has ever been given concerning the events of that weekend.

Consider the absence of the dead body of Jesus. The rumour was spread that his disciples had stolen the corpse, but no-one was ever able to prove it. If only the Jews could have produced the body, the dangerous rumour of his return to life could have been scotched once and for all. But the body had disappeared.

Think of the transformation of the discouraged band of followers – defeated by the execution of their Leader one day, and overwhelmed with such excitement a few days later that they risked their lives to spread the news. And that excitement was not reserved for the immediate disciples. It constitutes even today the basis for the faith of millions who make up the church. 'Christ is risen. He is risen indeed!'

Intelligent analysis

Throughout history millions of people have looked at the claims of Jesus and found that under the microscope they do make sense. A lot of those people have been intelligent, well educated and not easily hoodwinked. Some of them have started out with deliberately hostile intentions.

C. S. Lewis, professor of Medieval and Renaissance English at Cambridge University until his death in 1963, described himself as 'perhaps ... the most dejected and reluctant convert in all England' when in 1929 he 'gave in, and admitted that God was God, and knelt and prayed'.[100] Here was a brilliant and open mind that could no longer refute the evidence and was unwilling to be dishonest concerning what he found.

> I was by now too experienced in literary criticism to regard the gospels as myths ... And no person was like the Person it depicted; as real, as recognisable, through all that depth of time, as Plato's Socrates or Boswell's Johnson ... yet also

numinous, lit by a light from beyond the world, a god. But if a god ... then not a god, but God.[101]

If we are crying out for answers to unanswered questions and someone comes along with answers that make sense, it is worth stopping to listen to what he has to say. The biggest problem that most of us face is an instinctive and insistent assumption that such claims are impossible. We are prejudiced by our environment, which tells us that certain things cannot be – they are 'unscientific', unreasonable, imaginary. Sometimes our private moral agendas resist their implications.

The moral dilemma

In today's secular environment it is easy to jump to quick conclusions and then to cling to them as though our lives depended on it. One such conviction is that miracles cannot happen and unusual phenomena must have rational explanations. Either there is an explanation, or they are impossible. Virgins cannot give birth to babies, and therefore the conception of Jesus in a virgin is impossible. Miracles do not, indeed cannot, happen; there must be an explanation. The resurrection was a 'conjuring trick with bones', as one notorious bishop claimed.

The apostle Paul pre-empted modern sceptics when he said: 'If there is no resurrection of the dead, then not even Christ has been raised.' Q.E.D. It is the kind of rational logic that causes millions to make mockery of Christianity today. 'But,' he continued with absolute conviction, 'Christ has indeed been raised from the dead.'[102] Astonishing it may be, because it contradicted the assumptions of the day. But demonstrably true nevertheless.

How we fear the implications of admitting that the impossible just might have happened. That is exactly what the Christian faith asks of us. We peer into the fog that is called God and are comfortable with its mystery because it makes no demands upon us. Then in an extraordinary, belief-stretching way, the fog takes shape in a form that makes sense to us. 'Hang on,' we want to say, 'I can live comfortably with a God I can't understand. But this Jesus – if he really is God – brings the implications of deity uncomfortably close.'

I remember well the struggle I faced as it dawned on me that Jesus Christ could really be God and the gospel could really be true – knowing that, if that was the case, I was on the wrong side of the fence. John Stott in his evangelistic addresses to the university touched on this dilemma. My memory goes back forty years to his message in which he said that the world is full of those who like to believe in God but are reluctant to accept the consequences. Intellectual convictions often clash with moral inclinations, but we cannot forever sit on the fence.

If Jesus Christ is really divine, and if he is truly the doorway to God – and the evidence points clearly to both – then that has huge implications, not only for our morality, but for the whole way in which we conduct our lives. It is only the cowardly who cannot face up to that conclusion.

8

Only One Way
Don't all roads lead to heaven?

I lay in a hospital bed in New Delhi with hepatitis. I had got over the worst of the illness and was actually enjoying my stay in hospital. It gave me the excuse to lie around and do very little that I didn't want to do. I read a lot, ate a lot and slept a lot, while my co-workers were out in the heat and the sweat of the Indian summer. There were three others in the small ward, and a new patient had just joined us. He was a well-educated Indian and he was not too ill to talk. He asked me what I did, and very soon we were talking about religion. I told him that Jesus Christ had said, 'I am the way and the truth and the life. No-one comes to the Father except through me.'[103] So I clearly affirmed that he was the only way to God. 'Jesus Christ is unique,' I insisted. 'There is no other way we can come to God except through him.'

However ill my fellow patient may have been, he certainly was not too ill to get very angry with me, accusing me of arrogance, narrow-mindedness, prejudice – not to mention a heavy hang-over from colonialism. Was it any surprise that he should be offended when I was being so 'arrogant'?

This mosquito buzzes regularly in my ear:

How can we continue to make this exclusive claim to the truth? Even some churches have bowed to 'tolerance' and are inviting Hindus and Muslims to 'worship' in united services. Surely God is big-hearted enough to accept anyone who believes sincerely in whatever religion they were brought up in! Or is God really as narrow-minded and prejudiced as most Christians are?

Such bigotry means that there will be very few who are saved in the end. Heaven will look like a half-empty cathedral on a Sunday morning, and hell will look like an over-subscribed rock concert full of sincere people who just happened to believe the wrong thing. Come on ... be reasonable!

This is one of the greatest challenges to our faith today. Christianity has been widely accused of intolerance, and the modern world, which counts tolerance as one of its cardinal values, is deeply intolerant of Christianity's exclusive claims. Bible-believing Christians are made to look bigoted and 'broad-minded' modernists have laid claim to the moral high ground. And yet this exclusiveness is at the very heart of my claim to be a professing Christian – and even more, a missionary.

The problem of truth

Of course, we are not the only ones to lay claim to absolute truth and get tarred as intolerant, and other world religions with exclusive claims tend to get labelled in the same way. Islam must figure as one of the world's more 'intolerant' faiths. Witness the fallen Taliban regime in Afghanistan that went to extreme lengths to be faithful to the teachings of their prophet and their holy book. Consistency to their convictions compelled them to require Hindus to wear a distinctive mark on their clothing and to vow to kill anyone who converted to Christianity. It would be a mistake to hold up the Taliban as a model of Muslim consistency, but one must admire them for trying in the face of world criticism. Islam does make exclusive claims no less than Christianity.

The modern world gives a name to those who make these claims, and it has become a mark of disdain. Those who live by the fundamental tenets of their faith have come to be known as 'fundamentalists'. It was originally a title of honour, implying conviction and credibility. But today, rather like the word 'gay', it has been hijacked and deprived of its original meaning. A fundamentalist is now regarded as a bigot, prejudiced and intolerant of other creeds. It conjures up images of ranting mullahs, stave-wielding sadhus and Bible-waving tele-evangelists.

The word 'tolerance' has gone through a similar sea-change. Once upon a time tolerance implied the willingness to respect the beliefs and convictions of sincere people, without necessarily agreeing with them or being convinced by them. Today, tolerance has come to mean acceptance of every creed as of equal value – anything less is regarded as bigotry and prejudice. Josh McDowell calls this the 'New Tolerance':

> Today's doctrine of tolerance ... goes far beyond the dictionary's definition of tolerance. Webster's defines *tolerate* as 'to recognize and respect [others' beliefs, practices, etc.] without sharing them' ... But that's not what the word means any more ...
>
> The new tolerance is defined as the view that all values, beliefs, lifestyles, and truth claims are equal. In the words of Edwin J. Delattre, dean of Boston University's School of Education, the new tolerance involves 'the elevation of all values and beliefs to [a position worthy of equal] respect'.[104]

In a *Sunday Telegraph* review of the excellent Channel 4 series by David Frost on the Alpha course at Holy Trinity Church, Brompton, John Preston produced this worn cliché that typifies the new doctrine: 'There seem to be all sorts of reasons for not joining Alpha. Like all fundamentalist sects, it preaches intolerance.'[105] And that was a review of a programme that bent over backwards to emphasize that they were not forcing anything on anyone!

Whereas tolerance once meant that everyone had a right to his or her own beliefs, today tolerance implies that everyone's belief is equally true – except, of course, the beliefs of the 'fundamentalists'. It implies a huge shift in meaning. What has really changed is the perception of truth, one of the greatest casualties of today's world. It used to be said that if something was true, the opposite was therefore untrue; post-modernism has changed all of that. Now, what one person perceives as true may not necessarily be true for someone else. Absolute truth is in the casualty ward.

As Christians who believe that the Bible is God's Word, we have to reject the philosophy of the day and cling to absolute truth. In doing so, we do no less than the prophets and apostles of biblical times.

When the apostle Paul walked up the dusty road into Athens, he found himself surrounded by a plethora of deities – all competing for equal respect and allegiance. Had he been a post-modern apostle, he might have been content to set up a statue to Jesus alongside the road as just one more claim to truth. There are Hindu temples today where the picture of Jesus has joined the other gods in that sort of manner. But Paul could not do that. He declaimed his conviction of absolute truth and the unique superiority of Jesus Christ:

> The God who made the world and everything in it is the Lord of heaven and earth and does not live in temples built by hands ... We should not think that the divine being is like gold or silver or stone ... For he has set a day when he will judge the world with justice by the man he has appointed. He has given proof of this to all men by raising him from the dead. [106]

Paul's claim to the uniqueness of Jesus caused a riot, but that didn't alter the truth of what he preached. He affirmed it again towards the end of his long and controversial career, when he wrote that God 'wants all men to be saved and to come to a knowledge of the truth. For there is one God ...' That alone is an audacious claim, but it is not all. 'There is one God (*only one God*) and one mediator (*only one mediator*) between God and men, the man Christ Jesus ...' [107]

God wants all people to be saved?

In the course of my conversation with the Hindu gentleman in the Delhi hospital, he proposed the old analogy, 'All roads lead to Rome', in defence of his pluralism. It sounds so reasonable, so modern, so fair and understandable. It would be much more convenient to believe it – which perhaps explains its popularity. But the logic is flawed. Christians who remain loyal to the Bible cannot agree, because it quite simply isn't true.

'Sir,' I said. 'We are here in Delhi, and we want to get to Calcutta. However, we have to choose very carefully by which road we leave the city, or which train or plane we catch, because they do not all go to Calcutta. If we get on the wrong train, we will end up in Madras or Bombay. All roads do not lead to Rome. Many roads go elsewhere.' It is exactly what Jesus said:

> Enter through the narrow gate. For wide is the gate and broad is the road that leads to destruction, and many enter through it. But small is the gate and narrow the road that leads to life, and only a few find it.[108]

The mind of modern humanity (and my mind also) rebels against that statement, because it seems so unfair.

The world is a huge place. We are talking about six billion people, all of them brought up in their own culture, religion or superstition. If I am a Christian, I have to admit that I started out with a very unfair advantage. My mother and father were Christian, they took me to church and sent me to Sunday School, I was surrounded by Christians. I never seriously considered becoming a Buddhist. If I had been brought up in a Buddhist home, I probably would never have considered becoming a Christian.

I acknowledge that I would have no excuse before God if I was following the wrong path and he showed me clearly what was the true path to take. However, multiple millions of people in the world today (not to speak of the multiple millions in previous generations) have never had the option to know that they are wrong. Millions have never heard of Jesus Christ and do not know that he is the only way to approach God.

It is so easy, living in Britain and surrounded by signs of the Christian faith, to put the blame on people for not listening. Britain may no longer be a Christian country, but monuments and memories of the Christian faith are embedded in our culture – churches and cathedrals on the street corner, *Songs of Praise* on TV, Christmas carols in the High Street and Bibles in our local bookshop. No-one in Europe or America will be able to claim ignorance on the Last Day. But more than half the world does not have those privileges. They will be able to claim ignorance.

I remember my early experiences of preaching to a bazaar crowd in India. I got used to it after a while, but the first few times were unnerving. I travelled with my team – mostly Indian young men – in an old four-ton delivery van. When we came to a local market, we would park in a crowded area, drop the tailgate and stand on it with a small hand-held mike. From the vantage point of this raised platform I would look out over the crowd. We would start to sing a song and then begin to preach. Very quickly a huge mass of people would gather around and stare. The presence of one white-skinned foreigner was a bonus attraction.

If I were to do that in England I would at best get a couple of old people looking on in sympathy. If I were fortunate I might get a few insults, though the average English person is usually too polite or indifferent even to pause, let alone embarrass himself or herself by a stray comment.

But India is different. India is a land of people, most of whom have time to think, time to listen, time to talk. As I would stand up on the tailgate of the truck looking out over the crowd, I would have the attention of at least several hundred people fixed on me. And the thoughts that went through my mind over and over again were something like this:

These people – maybe five hundred, maybe a thousand – are probably all Hindus or Muslims. Most of them have probably never heard of Jesus Christ before, though the Muslims might have been taught that he was a prophet, but less important than Mohammed. Most of them will not understand what I am talking about, but this is possibly the first and last time they will ever hear about Jesus and his death on the cross.

What is God going to say to them at the Judgment Day? Will he say, 'You had a chance to believe in me and you turned me down. Go to hell'? What will he say to them? Who will be held responsible on the Last Day?

Sometimes we would ask village people if they had heard of Jesus Christ. Many times we would get no answer or a shrug of the shoulder. Was he a politician? Or a big landowner? A local businessman? Or a film star? In India alone there are today several hundred million who have no idea who Jesus Christ is, and in the whole world there are probably more than two billion.

Probably the most disturbing fact in this discovery is that most Christian people either don't know what is going on in the world, or don't really care. Or else they don't really believe that Jesus Christ is in fact the only way to God. This can be very confusing and troubling to those who take a little time to think it through. I have discerned a few common reactions to these awesome thoughts.

- Most common, of course, is for people not to think very deeply about these problems. Dale Carnegie[109] said that the average person is more troubled by his or her own headache than by a thousand people killed in an earthquake in China. That is either because we are all so selfish that it comes naturally to us, or God has mercifully spared us the consequences of thinking too deeply.

- Some people do think it through and find it too much to accept at face value. So they come to the conclusion that the Bible must be unreliable and the Christian message obviously untrue. People easily lose their faith over this problem, which unfortunately puts them in a much worse dilemma, as there is no better alternative. When faith dies, hope dies also.

- Others take a leap in the dark – the twenty-first-century solution – and end up with a pluralistic notion that Jesus is just one truth among many truths. In spite of the clarity of Jesus' words, they blandly affirm, he was just opening one door, but there are many other doors by which others can enter. Many people are good at turning black into white if it helps them to find a way out of the dilemma.

- Then there are the conscientious theologians who manage to conclude that Jesus cannot have meant exactly what he is recorded to have said. I can have some sympathy for them, even if they are hard to agree with in detail. No truly compassionate person can, without a tear, accept the traditional hard teaching on hell and consign the majority of humanity to eternal punishment.

Taking the bull by the horns

This is one of the greatest dilemmas of the Christian faith, and any Christian is not thinking very deeply if he or she has not sometimes stumbled over it. If I am to keep my faith with any real integrity, I must find some answers. I cannot accept any of the normal responses outlined above.

My faith is unfortunately too cerebral to be able to push the problem permanently out of sight and imagine that it does not exist. I believe, for reasons I have already stated, that the Bible is true and reliable. I cannot pretend that the verses I don't like are wrong and only the nice ones are true. Nor can I turn black into white at the wave of a wand and pretend that Jesus did not make exclusive claims. The Bible is far too clear about this and it takes enormous dishonest manipulation to believe otherwise.

I accept that sometimes the Bible has been harshly misinterpreted and we need to take a sympathetic look at some of its teachings for a better understanding. But honesty requires that we be wary of twisting the Scriptures till we can get them to agree with what we deem to be acceptable.

The problem of hell

We have touched on the problem of hell, and now we must examine it a little more closely. It is one of the more difficult aspects of Christian teaching, but it cannot be avoided.

At the outset it must be stated that there are many strange and unacceptable conceptions of hell. All those images of demons with black horns and pitchforks have given hell a bad name, and we need to clear them from our minds. C. S. Lewis did the Christian world a great service with his allegory *The Great Divorce*, in which he describes hell in terms of a vast, grey city where bickering, selfish people live out their miserable, endless lives in interminable tedium. But that too is inadequate to explain what the Bible tells us.

What is clear is that Gehenna, the Bible's word for hell (so called because it takes its name from the Jerusalem rubbish dump in the valley of Hinnom), is:

- A place of endless torment and sorrow, to be feared and avoided at any cost.
- A lake of fire and sulphur[110] and outer darkness.[111] (How can the two be reconciled? The description must be symbolic.)
- A place not originally prepared for humans but for the devil and his angels.[112]
- The destiny of the wicked and rebellious, who are not admitted to the city of God but remain outside its walls forever.[113]

John Stott made himself notorious for a while for having speculated about annihilation rather than endless torment in his book *Essentials: A Liberal–Evangelical Dialogue*, in which he and a liberal theologian, David Edwards, tackle each other's views on a number of difficult issues. Stott was spurred on by the accusation that Evangelicals liken God to an 'Eternal Torturer' who sadistically inflicts pain and consigns people to eternal fire. He demonstrates great compassion as he struggles with the traditional understanding of Gehenna:

> I want to repudiate with all the vehemence of which I am capable the glibness, what almost appears to be the glee, the *Schadenfreude*, with which some Evangelicals speak about hell.[114]

He admits – and with this we can surely all identify – that emotionally he finds the concept of eternal conscious torment for the unsaved intolerable. 'But our emotions are a fluctuating, unreliable guide to truth and must not be exalted to the place of supreme authority in determining it.'[115] Well said.

He then goes on to offer a case, from the Bible, for the ultimate annihilation – extinction to non-existence – of those who have not made their peace with God. I can sympathize with John Stott's (and all Christians') dilemma, and am convinced that emotionally he is absolutely right to struggle as he does with the concept of hell.

However, having longed to follow Stott's conclusions (and even he admits that he only holds his position tentatively), I am obliged to concede that the Scriptures remain uncomfortably clear about the reality of a place of 'eternal punishment',[116] where the beast and the false prophet will be 'tormented day and night for ever and ever'.[117] That same place is the lake of fire, and after the final judgment, 'if anyone's name was not found written in the book of life, he was thrown into the lake of fire'.[118] The conclusions seem unavoidable. How can we reconcile that with a God who claims that he does not want any to perish?

No easy answers

What enables me to cling to faith is the conclusion that, though there are no easy answers, I am convinced that the answers exist.

- There is sufficient lack of clarity in the teaching about hell in the Bible that absolute dogmatism would be unwise and careless. It is clear that a place of punishment is prepared for the utterly wicked and deliberately rebellious – and that squares easily with the justice of God. What is much less clear is the fate of those who have never had the opportunity deliberately to reject the gospel. I am very willing to give God the benefit of my doubt.
- Before I gave my life to Christ, and when I knew I was deliberately avoiding him, I played with the teachings of

Herbert W. Armstrong. Armstrong produced an attractive magazine and a lot of free literature, which propagated some strange and unorthodox teaching. Among other things he taught that after death unbelievers would be annihilated. I was immensely comforted by this teaching. It reassured me that, though I would never experience the enjoyment of heaven, I would at least be unaware of what I was missing. That in itself justifies the Bible's teaching on hell, and that is how Jesus so often applied it – as a warning to the careless and the deliberately rebellious.

- A far clearer truth that we can be absolutely sure of is that God is totally just. He will never do anything that is partial or unfair. What is more, he will do nothing that is not characterized by love, for his nature is love. How I can reconcile that with eternal punishment is not my problem, nor will it ever be. I do not have to sit upon the throne of final judgment. But I can trust him to do his difficult duty well.

The wider context

These arguments apply to the wider complex questions regarding the exclusive claims of Christ and the fate of millions who have never had an opportunity to know. There are mysteries that are too deep for us to look into. It would be surprising if it were otherwise.

Richard Wurmbrand, the Romanian pastor imprisoned by the Communists for many years for his faith, used to mock the claim of Yuri Gagarin, Russia's first astronaut, that he had been up in space and saw no signs of God. 'If an ant crawled around the rim of my shoe,' he would say, 'he would also claim he saw no sign of Wurmbrand.' In the claims of exclusiveness that the Bible appears to make, we are touching the sort of mystery that finite beings will do well to treat with humility and some ignorance. The measure of our understanding is very limited.

God is eternal and we are very temporal. God has a vast perspective, while we can only peer over the horizon. How dare we claim to understand all the mysteries of the universe? Scripture gives us some great insights into the mysteries of God, but it only reveals a fraction of what is in his mind. How dare we draw too many conclusions from the little we have been allowed to see?

This is what it means to live by faith – to believe with absolute confidence, and in the face of accusations to the contrary, that God is just and righteous. That is one of the primary revelations of the Scriptures. God can be trusted, and his creatures will never be able to take him to task for his treatment of them. His justice will never give greater punishment than we deserve – and his love and compassion have provided a way whereby he will not only withhold deserved justice, but is willing to give salvation to all who call on him. Is that too hard to cling to in the light of all we know about him?

And the fate of millions who have never heard the message of salvation? We need to cast that back on the One who initiated the problem. He made them, he has told us he does not want any of them to be lost, and he will have to judge them with absolute fairness on the Last Day. We must trust that he knows what he is doing. He is very capable, conscientious and compassionate.

Having said that, remember that God has clearly told us his plan in the matter. 'Go into all the world and preach the good news to all creation.'[119] We are not without responsibility, and we cannot blame God for not telling us his solution to the problem.

9

Sums That Don't Add Up
Can this be the Bride of Christ?

The church is surely one of the world's oddest institutions – to the outsider it looks like a social club with exclusive but supposedly open membership, whose subscribed and initiated members gather for strange rituals every Sunday and sometimes at other times as well.

One of the first things I discovered after I gave my life to Christ was that I had not just had my sins forgiven and gained eternal life. I had obtained access to a whole new culture, which I now needed to discover and master. Fortunately I was highly motivated and regarded it as a great privilege to belong to this community. It was just one of many interesting perks of my exciting commitment to Jesus Christ. I wasn't complaining, and I set out with resolute determination to master the insider secrets of this strange new society.

One of the first things to strike me was the odd addiction to abbreviations. The Christian club I had joined seemed to have its own specialist language. I would be asked if I was having a good 'QT' every morning – short for a 'Quiet Time' or morning Bible reading and prayer. I adopted the terminology and set out with some enthusiasm to master the language. There were some secrets to having a good QT. It was advisable to find a closet (a new meaning for a familiar word), where I would not be disturbed, and to use SU or IVP[120] notes. I was now welcome to attend the regular CU meetings – the Christian Union, which met weekly for a PM (prayer meeting) where we prayed for the CIM and BMMF[121] and occasionally for the RCs.[122] Initiation into this world of abbreviations was confusing, and that was before I had begun to understand the Songs of Zion and the significance of the blood and the atonement. It all fascinated me and made me feel I had a lot to catch up on before I could feel fully integrated into this unusual community. But there was a great sense of belonging once I had mastered the code.

Then, of course, there were the cultural rules. I used to think that these were sacred and Bible-based guidelines, but have since discovered that a lot of this is shifting sand. Firstly, I was very happy to discover that 'Christians don't dance'. Relief! I hated dancing with a passion, ever since the days when mother forced me to go to the Women's Institute Christmas dance in the village hall. I have since discovered that Christians organize barn dances and even go to discos, and that the Bible is pretty silent on the subject.

Smoking was out for Christians. I smoked my last fag the night before I gave my life to Christ, though I played with a pipe for a while after that, until I read 1 Corinthians. 'Come back to your senses as you ought, and stop sinning.'[123] I gave up immediately. And then I attended an IVF missions conference and found all the Dutch Christians smoking like a house on fire. I was mystified.

Drinking was more straightforward. I used to do some light social pub-crawling (normal life for Dublin University students) until I was saved. That all changed in the new community. I became teetotal. And then, a few years on, I visited the home of Ian, a Christian friend who was in the process of examining and shifting his cultural traditions. He called his new discovery 'freedom from law'. This was truly complex. There on the dinner table was a bottle of wine. It stood as a challenge to my cultural assumptions, a test to see if I was truly free or still in bondage.

My friend had another test to put me through. In my Christian culture we took it for granted that before eating we said a prayer. When we sat down for this meal, Ian began with a challenge: 'If you're thankful, go ahead and eat.' No closing of the eyes, no ritual murmured appreciation.

I was stunned. What was I supposed to do? Was that his way of saying, 'In our house we don't give thanks for the food'? Should I comply? Or was it his way of saying, 'If you are still in bondage to old traditions, say your own prayer'? I was confused – and I am sure I proved to Ian that I was still a traditionalist and in bondage. I prayed my own prayer of thanks, and then enjoyed the food. I don't remember if I drank the wine.

The church – strange new world

Many people have raised these questions and looked with wonder on the claim that the local parish church is the Bride of Christ, which Christ loved and for which he died. Many books are in circulation that mock the follies of church culture, and I don't need to add to their insights.

But the questions remain. I have visited many churches all over the world, of all kinds of denominations, and there are many different flavours. Some are unbelievably boring and irrelevant. Some still chant in medieval languages and others have exciting music and people who dance and shout. They all use a distinctive vocabulary and intonation and do strange and distinctive things.

Some churches totally ignore newcomers (which sometimes is a relief); others make awkward approaches to indicate that they don't want to be unfriendly – but they don't want to get too close either. Some press you to indulge in doughnuts and coffee before the service as if to prove that worship and consumption are not mutually exclusive. Few churches succeed in making anyone feel truly 'at home' on their first attempt. Is this really God's temple?[124]

Chuck Swindoll observes that in his view

> churches need to be less like national shrines and more like local bars ... less like untouchable cathedrals and more like well-used hospitals, places to bleed in rather than monuments to

look at ... places where you can take your mask off and let your
hair down ... places where you can have your wounds dressed.

He then quotes a friend of his, a converted Marine:

... the only thing I miss is that old fellowship all the guys in
our outfit used to have down at the slop shoot ... we'd sit
around, laugh, tell stories, drink a few beers, and really let our
hair down. It was great!

But now I ain't got nobody to tell my troubles to, to admit
my faults to. I can't find anybody in church who will put their
arms around me and tell me I'm still okay. Man, it's kinda
lonely in there![125]

Sometimes the church looks like a variety of social club with
some unusual habits. It has been referred to as a unique tribe
with its own indigenous rituals and taboos. Dave Tomlinson,
one of the leaders of the 'New Church' movement in Britain in
the 1970s and 1980s, was disturbed by the narrow-minded
church culture that closed the doors to many serious searchers
for God. His book, *The Post Evangelical*, raised a few eyebrows
when it was published in 1995. In it he investigated the issue of
the church's cultural image:

Middle-class evangelicals ... identify Christianity with the
standards, values and attitudes of their own culture: in this
case, middle-class culture ... The consequence of confusing
Christianity with middle-class values is that people who do
not identify with that culture reject the church, and, in many
cases, the gospel too.[126]

Tomlinson's solution was to start a different kind of church,
facetiously called 'Holy Joe's' and meeting, predictably, in the
lounge bar of a south London pub on Tuesday nights. Why a
pub? For the same reasons as Ian put wine on the table when he
invited me to dinner – it shocks the traditionalists. Why
Tuesday night? Any night but Sunday would do. 'I believe,' he
says, 'Holy Joe's has demonstrated the possibilities of an
alternative church life.'[127]

He doesn't have everything right and I keep the book on a shelf I reserve for risqué titles – 'to be treated with caution'. But he is asking good questions and proposing some interesting if controversial answers.

So this is the church?

One Christmas during my years in India, I arrived with my team at a small town in Uttar Pradesh, to the south of Varanasi. We were there for a week or two of evangelism and meetings and had made advance arrangements with the local church. They should have been expecting us, but we were not prepared for what we found. We visited the little church building, standing gauntly in a bare patch of ground some distance from the town. It had been decorated for Christmas with faded coloured streamers.

Tragedy had struck just two days earlier. The Christians had been feuding for some time over the mission property, and the congregation was deeply divided by greed and envy. Some members of one party had come to the church building and found a member of the opposition hanging up paper decorations. They had argued, picked a quarrel and beaten the poor man to death. Just before we arrived, five of the church's elders had been arrested and were now in prison awaiting trial on a charge of murder.

It caught me off guard with an extraordinary intensity. For days I battled doubt – questioning the church (for which Christ died), the authenticity of the Christian faith (which promised victory over the evil one), and the promises of God (that he would save to the uttermost).

Was it all worthwhile, this sacrifice of my life for his cause? Or was the Christian gospel an empty sham? Were the Christians any better, any holier, than the non-Christian community around them? Or was it all a big game and not worth a lifetime of sacrifice?

The Christian faith makes many claims about the power of God to change lives. In fact it is one of its most basic claims that if we

come to Christ in repentance and faith, our lives will be renewed.
The church of redeemed people is supposedly God's greatest and most
beautiful creation. So what do we make of what we see in the
church? Is it idle dreaming with no basis in reality?

Serious claims and solemn questions.

As leader of my team, I was obliged to say and do the right
thing, to build up and not to tear down; but privately I also had
to face up to the fact that my beliefs were under severe strain.
Those mosquitoes were buzzing in my head. It forced me for a
while into a double life – a public face of faith and an inner
battle with doubt. It is the dilemma faced by many sincere
Christians. Some come through it triumphantly, some succumb
to cynicism, some bury their heads in the sand and hope for the
best, and some retreat in disarray.

One special problem made my life even harder at that time. I
had recently picked up and read a copy of David Shub's
biography of V. I. Lenin, leader of the 1917 Bolshevik revolution in Russia.[128] If there was one thing that struck me forcibly
about his story, it was that he was at least consistent to his
beliefs.

Lenin was a materialist and an atheist. He firmly and
decisively rejected any concept of God or the supernatural,
invisible world. In his eyes the Bible was a pack of lies and a
human fabrication. Human destiny was clearly in human hands.
The way he behaved, ruthlessly eliminating people who stood in
the way of his ideals as though they were material objects
without dignity or value, was entirely consistent with his belief
system.

How easy it was for Lenin to be consistent! He even insisted
that his bodily remains should not be preserved to be worshipped
like a god – how inconsistent are his followers who revere his
corpse to this day! It was this quality of consistency that I found
attractive – and the inconsistency of the Christians of that little
Indian town that I found so unattractive.

Another incident in India stands out in my mind. I had
preached in a small church in central Uttar Pradesh. Right after

the service, the congregation filed out into the sunshine and stood around in front of the church door. Above the door was an inscription that read 'United Church of North India'. Within two minutes of the close of the service, two church members started to argue outside the church. It was more than an argument. They bared their fists and were soon at each other, out to draw blood. It would have made a marvellous photo, with the inscription over the church door behind these fighting Christians. 'By this all men will know that you are my disciples, if you love one another.'[129]

If there is any one thing that demonstrates the unreality and irrelevance of the Christian faith, surely it is the inconsistent behaviour of Christian people, the extraordinary dichotomy between what we say we believe and the way we behave. To this alone must be credited the departure of millions from the faith.

I could slide further down this slippery slope if I chose, with a long list of Christian failings. The media delights to highlight the hypocrisy of the saints. There is scant newsworthy value, and little surprise, if a screen star – or even a politician – has a sordid adulterous affair. But catch an evangelist or a vicar in a compromising scandal, and it makes the headlines. We can draw some comfort from the fact that the world expects something better of Christians.

How can we learn to live with this catalogue of failure? Or, to rephrase the question, should we learn to live with it? Would it not be more honest to admit that the Christian faith is full of promise, but it just doesn't work in reality? Just look at the church to see whether it works. That, unfortunately, is what so many people do, and we can't blame them when they conclude that it is irrelevant or a crutch for the emotionally inadequate.

Jesus said that the church is his body. If the world wants to know what Jesus' body is like, they are invited to look at us and to judge him by what they see. That is an awesome responsibility and we sadly and regularly fail to live up to expectations.

Getting back onto solid ground

Looking back at those crisis days I passed through in 1968, when I found Lenin more attractive and more consistent than the church, I am today grateful for the lessons I learned in that experience. The first lesson was one of perspective.

It is a cliché to say that you cannot see the wood for the trees, but it is true nonetheless. Close up to the event, one can only see the problems: a murdered man, Christians in disarray, a church in disgrace. It was a depressing sight, and if that were all I could see, I would hold out little hope. But let us step back a little in time and space. What do I see now?

A whole world in disarray

Firstly, I see something depressingly normal. What is so unusual about a murder, hatred, bitterness and people fighting over their petty 'rights' and privileges? Sadly, nothing unusual. It is the tragic stuff of the world of men and women. What is really amazing is that there is a company of people in the midst of the mess who are not supposed to be, and not expected to be, fighting among themselves. That says something important about the church. It is supposed to be different and we are sick at heart when it isn't.

A people of faith and hope

Now what is faith? Faith has never been mistaken for perfection, and a people of faith have never pretended to be without fault. The people of faith are those who know that things should be different – and one day will be different. Faith lives next door to hope and love.

Lenin may have behaved in a way consistent with his principles. His principles told him that there is no world above, no hope for a future paradise, no faith in a deity who cares. His principles told him that he could kill human beings if it advanced his cause, and it would matter no more than swatting a fly because it irritated him. Lenin might well have lived a life consistent with his materialist, atheistic creed, and the bloody history of the Soviet Union testifies to the barren outcome of his consistent life.

Many Christian people live inconsistent lives. They flounder and fail, they disgrace their cause and dishonour their Master. But isn't that just the message of the Bible repeated over and over? The Old Testament is a story of regular failure, and God stood patiently by to pick up the pieces, coax them back to repentance and encourage them never to lose hope. Simon Peter blew it when he denied Christ at his trial, and he wept bitterly. Thank God that there is space for some failures and hypocrites in the company of the people of faith.

A standard of perfection

This was the truth that helped me back onto my feet. While I could so easily and thoroughly be disillusioned with the people of God, I found I could never be disappointed in Jesus Christ. It is only natural to want and need people to look up to, people who will be models and examples for us. We all have our heroes about whom we fancy there can be no fault. What folly! The world of faultless heroes is a fictitious world, and the longer we live, the more our heroes crumble and fail.

One of my close friends and mentors in Pakistan, whose example and superior missionary experience I greatly admired, overthrew the Christian faith, committed adultery and left his wife for a younger woman. Another of my close Pakistani co-workers, whom I had trusted and relied upon, not only left his wife, but then converted to Islam and married his wife's sister. Should I be discouraged by that? Of course I should, and I was. But should I be surprised, or accuse God of failure? Of course not. People fail.

Look at the example of the greatest king of Israel, whose greater son was Jesus the Messiah. Did King David ever fail or disappoint his people? Not only did he commit adultery, but then went on to commit murder to cover up his sin. How could that be, when he was such a close friend of God? The lesson is clear: God is not surprised when his people fail, and neither should we be surprised. But we can both grieve.

But this great truth stands, of which we can be absolutely sure, that Jesus has never yet disappointed anyone. Look at him in the Scriptures. Whatever pressure he was subjected to, he remained without fault. People have been examining the record of his life and sayings for 2,000 years, and though many have attempted to attack and undermine him, he still has countless devotees who find no fault in him.

Hold on to these two great Bible truths:

- People are ultimately unreliable, and belong to a race that has fallen from perfection and is desperately in need of rescue.
- Jesus is utterly reliable, and no-one has yet found any fault in him.

God's peculiar people

The church is still a strange institution and has many faults. After twenty centuries of development and struggle, it is still full of failing human beings, rooted in their own small worlds. They are easy to laugh at, easy to make fun of, easy even to despise. They are a community that is hard to get into, sometimes hard to understand and very hard to change. But, wonder of wonders, God loves the church and plans one day to transform it and make it perfect. If that is not a wonderful message of grace, then what is?

Let us not despair, even if we don't understand. Let us not give up, even if it looks hopeless. Let us learn the language, adapt to the culture and laugh at our strange habits. And let us not criticize the church too harshly until we have looked closely into the hearts and motives of its members.

10

Over the Top
Christian dishonesty

About forty miles to the north of Lahore lies Pakistan's second city, Gujranwala, a town of about half a million inhabitants. It is a chaotic jumble of dusty dwellings, traffic and congestion, where horse-drawn carts, buffaloes and goats vie with rickshaws for dominance of the main road that runs through the centre.

For Christians it is significant as the location of several important Christian institutions. The Technical Training Institute has provided excellent courses for young Christians in a variety of disciplines from carpentry to draughtsmanship, and many have been trained for life there. The Gujranwala Theological Seminary has prepared generations of men to be pastors in the main denominations, and the United Bible Training Centre has done similar service for Christian women. There is a sizeable Christian population in Gujranwala.

A number of years ago a group of evangelists from overseas arrived in Gujranwala to hold meetings. This is quite a common thing in Pakistan. There is an annual 'Convention season' when most churches erect an open-air platform with loudspeaker equipment, and hundreds, sometimes thousands, of people come to attend lengthy gospel meetings.

I first came to know about this event when I read the magazine published by one of those invited preachers. This was his report on the meetings at which he spoke: 'Miracles in Pakistan! ... 10,000 Moslems receive Jesus Christ as their Saviour ... ' I could hardly believe what I read, as I know Pakistan well enough to know that this was either a phenomenal revival or a deceptive exaggeration.

Some time later I came across the magazine of a different evangelistic organization, and again the headlines screamed: 'Breakthrough in the Islamic World! ... 10,000 responded to know Jesus as their Saviour.' Could this be another revival? I investigated and wrote to both evangelists, and finally received reasonably friendly replies. The two reports were in fact of the same event at which both evangelists had spoken. The statistics they published were evidently given to them by their local hosts, and one of the men did acknowledge in his personal letter to me that 'we use such terms as "10,000 made a public stand" or "responded to the message of the Gospel" which is the truth. Only God knows how many were truly "BORN AGAIN" so we do not make such claims.' I urged caution and moderation in his reporting.

A year or two later, the same evangelist returned to Pakistan and conducted meetings in Karachi. This time his claims were even greater: 'Over 30,000 responded to receive Christ during the crusade.'

In reality all of these claims were of course grossly exaggerated. I have been in Gujranwala many times since then, and I know the churches and the local situation well. I have met with people who attended the meetings, and the translator for both evangelists is a close friend. It is possible that some people were healed and probably some nominal Christians gave their lives to Christ. Possibly even some Muslims put their faith in Christ also. There is, however, no evidence whatever of the impressive claims made by both these Christians leaders. The same is true of Karachi.

Sadly, this kind of false representation is extremely common among Christians. It presents a huge integrity problem.

The most valuable possession Christians have is the truth. And yet Christian people everywhere appear to throw away the truth for lesser values, such as credibility, donor support, popularity or an impression of blessing and power. Is this the church that Christ died for? Is this his Bride, filled with the Spirit of Truth?

In the film *Leap of Faith* Steve Martin acts the part of a travelling American evangelist who sets out deliberately to deceive the people who faithfully and hopefully flock to his tent to experience a 'miracle'. Night after night he manipulates the gullible crowd with smooth words, sentimental music and generated atmosphere. All along he is taking them for a ride. It is a take-off, of course, and there are not many charlatans on the stage who are quite so brazen in their deceit. But, tragically, it is too close to the truth for comfort.

Dressing up the flesh

There is another kind of Christian deceit that is perhaps even more dangerous, the kind that is at heart carnal but wears spiritual clothing. It promotes the flesh in the guise of spirituality, and is sometimes propagated by seemingly sincere people.

I think of an evangelist whom I know, a man who has preached the gospel to many and seen people turn to Christ. I have visited him in his home and listened to his preaching. I think of another friend in senior leadership in the church. I don't want to identify people and so the qualities I give below are a composite of several people I know. They are qualities all too common among God's people.

The man of faith and power

As soon as I step inside his home I am faced with a life-sized portrait of the evangelist in all his handsome splendour. He keeps it inside the front door so that no-one can miss it as they enter. There is even the hint of a halo around his head. It is clear that this is the image he wants to project of himself – a man of faith and power in whom the people can put their trust. He promotes himself, his achievements, his giftedness. He clearly believes he is a great man.

In his presentation from the platform (I have watched him on the stage in his expensive designer clothes) he emphasizes how much he has travelled, how many countries he has preached in and how widely he is recognized. How strange that people feel the need to boast about their travels, as though God specially honours the globe-trotter! If he has opportunity, he also makes sure we know how many radio or TV stations he can be heard and seen on.

He enjoys titles and boasts about his (probably unearned) qualifications. He has been duped by a quack institution that gives away degrees and doctorates for a fee – a small price to pay for the added respect that he gets from his admirers. One of my friends uses the 'Dr' before his name, and one day I asked him how he gained his doctorate.

'I studied part-time for two years,' he replied, 'and I wrote a thesis.'

'How long was your thesis?' I asked.

'Ten pages.' Such qualifications give no credit to those who work hard to earn their degrees and improve their abilities, but they do much to boost the faltering ego.

The lure of popularity

My evangelist friend loves the large crowds, the mega-church, and the mass adulation that goes with popular preaching. He likes to be in control of large numbers of people, and is often to be seen strutting about the stage like a caged lion, touching people here and there and drawing their adulation. He enjoys the atmosphere generated by persuasive music and clever words that can sway people to respond. He makes sure that he is the centre of attention, though he will often urge the people to give glory to God. He is a consummate performer.

The reports of his ministry never fail to present how mightily God is using him, and usually show him in centre stage surrounded by admirers to whom he is ministering. He is fond of statistics and makes good use of his cameraman. He loves to be seen as God's man of faith and power. His ego is fit to burst.

Many of his reports associate him with recognized Christian leaders. He will either be photographed beside them, be seen sitting on the platform with them or carry their commendations. He is a master of the art of associated credit, and he is a great name-dropper.

Perhaps the saddest thing of all is that such performers are often very popular. They know how to stir up a crowd, hold out promises to the hungry, and manipulate the hopeful.

Name it and claim it

This is the moment to touch on the so-called 'Health and Wealth Gospel' which, astonishingly, continues to lure people into believing that it is God's plan to give us everything we want. I am not a great student of this teaching, but I subscribe to some of the magazines of its popular proponents, and I browse their literature in order to know what they are offering. The materials are usually well produced, glossy and attractive and they exude positive faith.

It is easy to be blindly critical of those who hold out the promise of prosperity and miracles. There is a lot in their teaching that is excellent. The gospel they preach is positive and uplifting, and their emphasis on health and wealth for all is definitely preferable to the offerings of the 'sickness and poverty' brand of Christianity, which gives little hope short of heaven. If nothing else, positive expectation is good psychology and creates happier people.

In a recent magazine the lead article dealt with the dangers of stress. It was both biblical and helpful. But a few pages later in the same issue a banner headline proclaimed: 'Making God's Creative Power Work for You'. The title itself suggested a manipulation of God to suit our greed. And the article, by John Avanzani, confirmed the title:

So, you need a new car. You've been told to believe God for it ... you've been told all kinds of things to do to get it ... but how do you actually move it from that heavenly supply system into your driveway?![130]

The writer went on to tell us how we can speak out our faith and eventually manipulate God into working for us:

'But you'll never get a new car like that!' protest the unbelievers.

'Oh, no? You ought to see the new car I already got like that.'

This brand of 'faith teaching' makes a lot of bold, exciting and logical-sounding assertions, and it is no surprise that it is popular. Thousands throng to the conventions and eagerly grasp the promises. Millions in the Third World are drawn to the hope that some miracle can lift them above the poverty-line and save them from the fear of hunger and disease.

The logic is this. God is a God of love who desires nothing but good for his children. He has made a covenant to give us, by grace, everything that we need, including good health, freedom from all stress, worry and fear, and sufficient material provision to constitute the 'good life'. In fact he will withhold 'no good thing ... from those whose walk is blameless'.[131] Our role is simply to reach out in faith, believe that we have it, and it will be ours. It sounds good; it appears to be biblical, and in fact, *rightly understood*, it is true.

The problem begins when believers in need – whether suffering from illness, poverty, unemployment or any of a multitude of hardships – seeing the golden promise, believe that anything they want can be theirs if they only have the right kind of faith. I know a lady who was killed in a tragic accident. 'It would never have happened,' said a friend under the influence of health-and-wealth teaching, 'if she had claimed a long life in faith.'

There is a medicine so powerful it can cure every sickness and disease known to man. It has no dangerous side effects. It is safe even in massive doses. And when taken daily according to directions, it can prevent illness altogether and keep you in vibrant health. Does that sound too good to be true? It's not ... You don't have to call your doctor to get it. You don't even have to drive to the pharmacy. All you must do is reach for your Bible, open to Proverbs 4:20–24 and follow the instructions you find there.

When sickness attacks your body, you can tap into the healing Word you've put inside you and run that sickness off! Exactly how do you do that? You open your mouth and speak – not words of sickness and disease, discouragement and despair, but words of healing and life, faith and hope.[132]

So simple and so deceptive. And the same principle may equally be applied to all the other needs and problems of life. 'It is definitely God's will for all of his children to prosper!'[133] Believe and you will receive, and if you still don't seem to be getting what you want, just act as though you have it and keep on believing.

So what is wrong with this teaching? In brief, it doesn't work. It treats God as a slot machine, as an endless supply stream of everything we want, and his Word as the formula that will produce the goods. God and reality just do not operate like that. God's greatest desire for us is not that we should be happy, healthy and rich, but that we should be holy and blameless,[134] and sometimes he 'disciplines us for our good, that we may share in his holiness. No discipline seems pleasant at the time, but painful'.[135] The God of love sometimes causes us pain in order to be kind to us. Bible biography and church history bear out the reality of that. The ultimate promise of an 'inheritance ... in the kingdom of light'[136] where there shall be 'no more death or mourning or crying or pain' belongs to the future when 'the old order of things has passed away'.[137] The prosperity teachers have got some of the teaching right, but they have the timing badly wrong.

Their empty promises result in a lot of desperate and dis-illusioned people, either pretending they are healthy and wealthy because it would be unspiritual to act otherwise, or defeated and depressed because their faith does not appear to 'work' for them.

This so-called 'Word of Faith' teaching is essentially material-istic, greedy and presumptuous, postulating that every Christian has a right to success, prosperity and luxury in the here and now. Sometimes these preachers come to the Indian sub-continent. Staying in five-star hotels, they emerge to preach their hollow message to eager listeners, before retreating to their air-conditioned rooms and then returning back home before the true results of their ministry show up. It is a sham, and it leaves multitudes disappointed and disillusioned. It promises bread and gives a stone.

Listen to another brand of the same creed. I came across this advertisement in a free London paper. I do not think it is Christian – in fact I think its origin is more likely a crude offshoot of Islam – but it comes from the same stable as the Christian teachers we have just looked at:

> No matter what your problems are I can help to solve them. If you are a victim, I will break curses, protect you and destroy the powers of witchcraft, black magic, bad luck, and bring back loved ones. Your problems of marriage, sexual impot-ency, business careers, exams, court cases, will be solved. Pay after result.[138]

If I did not see through the fallacies of this teaching, it would quickly make me a cynic. I recognize that some prosperity teachers are sincere in their conviction that God wants to give his people a better deal. Others, however, are cynical manipulators of the Word of God, dishonestly twisting the truth to their own advantage. We all know who it is that benefits most from this false gospel – the ones who drive away in their Mercedes and strut the stage in their Gucci suits. That should make us angry.

The tragedy is that millions do not appear to have the discernment to understand that it is a false gospel. Many pin their hopes on a God who will solve all their problems and give them whatever they want in abundance. When they do not get what they have been promised, the result is either self-blame and discourage-ment, or a downward spiral into cynicism and unbelief.

OVER THE TOP 121

I am not going to lose my faith over dishonesty and greed in the church, nor does it undermine my confidence in the authenticity of the gospel. But it does often make me despair of the people of God, who are so easily duped and so easily led astray.

In contrast to the dishonesty and greed that is prevalent among God's people, thank God there is a godly alternative, which only serves to cast light on the phoney by highlighting the genuine.

The Servant of all

It was pride that first caused Adam and Eve to stumble and fall. They believed the nonsense that Satan propagated because it appealed to their egos. It is this arrogance that is so stunningly absent in Jesus.

Watch the Son of Man in the upper room on the night before his death. The disciples are gathered, all twelve of them including Judas, and the doors are locked. The flickering lights illumine their expectant faces. It is a dramatic moment at the end of an eventful, ominous day. They are locked away and alone now, and the Passover meal is spread before them.

Uncharacteristically, however, there are no servants to do the needful. The disciples look at each other expectantly, wondering which of them should do the menial job of washing their weary, dusty feet.

We all know what happened. To everyone's dismay and shame, Jesus got up from his place at the head of the table, took a towel and a basin of water and began to wash those twenty-four dirty feet. Only Peter had the courage to protest and acknowledge his humiliation: 'You shall never wash my feet.'[139] It was a brave gesture and Jesus overruled it. The lesson was clear:

> Now that I, your Lord and Teacher, have washed your feet, you also should wash one another's feet. I have set you an example that you should do as I have done for you.[140]

I contrast that with the smart-suited evangelist prancing across the stage in the floodlights, brimming with arrogance and assumed power: 'In the name of Jesus, touch her! I feel the power ...' He flings his arms dramatically in the air, while his admirers cry out for more.

B. R. Sircar

And then I think of an unassuming man of God, whom I knew in Calcutta many years ago. Bibu Ranjan Sircar was probably the most Christ-like person I had ever met. He dressed simply, travelled simply, lived simply. On those occasions when I slept in the same room as he, I would be aware that a great while before daybreak he was already on his knees, long before I was even able to drag myself from my bed.

B. R. Sircar lived in a simple bamboo home to the south of Calcutta, which he called Gospel Cottage. It was the base for his extensive travels – not across the world by jumbo jet, but throughout West Bengal by bus, second-class train and rickshaw and on foot. He was known in villages all over the state and welcomed by ordinary people wherever he went. Hundreds came to Christ and were discipled by his low-key, servant-like ministry.

I am sure he had faults, no doubt more than I ever came to know about. But the memory I have of him is marked by his humility and grace, gentleness and simplicity. Rare qualities indeed, but they surely reflect the personality of Christ, and they restore hope that true godliness has not been swallowed up by our obsession with size and glamour.

If pride is one of the ugliest and most deceitful temptations in Christian ministry, greed must run a close second – not just greed for money, but greed for power, for popularity and success, and sometimes greed to be known as a person of influence and power, all of which set out to tempt even the most sincere and committed believers. Examples of greedy people sadly spring to mind much more easily than do examples of simplicity and true godliness. But it is the godly few that restore our faith in the reality and relevance of the gospel.

Ramesh

Ramesh is a Nepali Christian friend whom I came to know when I lived in Nepal in the 1970s. He comes from an educated and cultured Hindu family and they were not impressed when he committed his life to Christ. Ramesh has a sharp and capable mind, which led him to study at Oxford University, where his impressive thesis on the parable of the wheat and the tares gained him a deserved Ph.D. He then returned to his country to serve the church.

Ramesh has written books and Bible commentaries, mostly in Nepali and for the use of the people he loves. After serving as principal of one of the first theological colleges in Kathmandu, he founded an accredited theological library, which serves almost all the Bible colleges in Nepal. No more than two or three Nepali Christians have earned so high an academic qualification from one of the world's leading universities, and there is ample scope for boasting or profiteering from the achievement, but Ramesh never flaunts his qualifications. His commitment to see the church in Nepal well grounded in the truth of Scripture is what motivates him, and his simple lifestyle demonstrates little interest in boasting in his achievements. While I can remember friends like Ramesh, I feel there is still hope for the church.

Robert Otto

For many years I counted as a close friend an elderly Pakistani clergyman, very well read and with a keen mind. Robert Otto was fluent in English, widely read in theology and a great admirer of John Stott, whose books I would try to provide for him. I first met Robert when he invited me to speak at a service he took every morning at five o'clock in a small church on the outskirts of Lahore for the workers in the brick kilns. One of the great ambitions of his life was to buy plots of land on which poor Christians could build places of worship, and he gave all the spare money he had from his inheritance and his small income for that purpose.

The last time I met Pastor Robert was at the local workshop where his second-hand motorcycle was being repaired. Well into his seventies, he had graduated from his battered bicycle on which for years he used to ride out to the villages to visit the poorest of the poor who worked in the brick kilns that surround the city. He died an unsung hero and passed on, largely unnoticed, to a well-earned and abundant reward, one of Pakistan's unique and rare saints. I have rarely met someone with a more unpretentious and generous spirit.

Samuel John

Samuel John became blind when he was still a young man as a result of a sports injury. When I met him he was already in his seventies and he lived in a poor quarter of Lahore and ruled his home with an iron fist. But it was not only his family that he cared for, in spite of his blindness. He opened his home to take in four or five poor Christian blind people, and he used his own meagre resources to teach them Braille and cane-work and to equip them for life. Samuel loved the Lord and we helped him to start a weekly worship service in his home, which was attended by the blind and the lame and a variety of other needy people in the neighbourhood. He assured us that he prayed for our 'long life and prosperity' every day of his life and we were humbled and enriched by his generosity and the simplicity of his life.

Heaven will surely be filled with people we won't recognize – not because we haven't seen them, but because they were so unassuming and so ordinary that we never noticed them. We were too dazzled by the glamour of the high-flyers. I suppose some of them will be in heaven too, but perhaps hidden away in a less prominent corner.

11

The World of Make-Believe
Christian fantasy

I can accept that there is hypocrisy in the Christian camp. Hypocrisy is the most biblical of sins, especially for religious professionals. Jesus faced it. Its existence didn't shake his faith and it shouldn't shake ours. In fact, the longer I profess to be a Christian, the more hypocrisy I find in myself.

I used to notice how often some preachers would repeat phrases such as, 'I am preaching this to myself as much as to anyone', 'I need this message as much as you', 'I also fail to live up to this standard' or words to that effect. In ignorant judgmentalism I used to think to myself, 'If they can't practise what they preach, why do they expect us to?'

I am wiser now than I used to be, and the more I understand of the Bible and the world, the more I realize that I am as inconsistent as anyone else. I know so much in my mind now, and every day that passes provides me with more knowledge – much of which I try to translate into understanding – and yet my life demonstrates so little of the fruits of this wisdom. The gulf between profession and practice widens, and it is distressing.

Perhaps it is for this reason that some professing Christians seek escape into Christian fantasy. A fantasy world provides an exciting escape when reality is hard to come to terms with. As if the truth were not fantastic enough, some Christians feel the need to invent even greater fantasies. Douglas Groothuis refers to the bumper sticker that reads: 'I've given up on reality. Now I'm looking for a good fantasy.'[141]

Take, for example, a project known as 'Operation Ice Castle',[142] an imaginative prayer journey to Nepal made by members of a reputable Prayer Network in September 1997. Such journeys for intercession have become popular in recent years and no doubt God has honoured the enthusiasm of these intercessors for the nations of the world. Prayer Networks form part of a rising tide of intercession in certain churches for some of the most spiritually needy places in the world, and they highlight the importance of prayer for the people of God. There is much in the movement that has resulted in positive blessing. But there is also much in the movement that borders on the fantastic. The tragedy is that Christians seem to be incapable of discerning between the genuine and the bizarre.

Under the name of Operation Ice Castle, two teams of intercessors arrived in Nepal and set out for Mount Everest, where they were convinced that the Queen of Heaven had her seat. One of the teams, based at the Everest base camp, set out for the mountain, evidently without experienced guides. They circulated a report of their experiences:

> After five days of prayer, on September 22, 1997, an incredible climbing anointing came over the team, and God led us through the Ice Fall, the most difficult, dangerous, and technically exacting part of the Everest ascent, with no guide but Him and no help other than from His angels. After many hours of crossing crevasses and climbing ice walls, we were about to reach the point where we had located the seat of the Queen of Heaven. At that moment the fury of the devil was unleashed and a huge avalanche broke loose above us, sending megatons of ice and snow crashing our way. At the last moment a huge crevasse in front of us swallowed up the avalanche, saved our lives, and we only had to deal with the [life-threatening] resulting cloud of ice for about ten minutes.

Apart from the folly of going into the dangerous Khumbu Icefall without guides, facing the threat of crevasses and avalanches, this report bears more of the marks of an excitable imagination than of reality. But that is only the beginning. The same evening, the report continues, God spoke to the team: 'Go out from this mountain tomorrow before 11:00 a.m. because I am going to destroy everything.' Then occurred what the report describes as 'the greatest avalanche ever seen in Everest. Base camp was totally buried under the snow' and a team of Koreans was killed.

Whatever we make of the accuracy of the report or the advisability of this kind of risky prayer trip, it is the deductions that concern us here. In consequence of the prayers of these two teams and the 'destruction of the throne of the Queen of Heaven', the intercessors pointed to certain catastrophic world events – in the words of the reporter, 'events ... which she senses have some connection':

- Huge fires broke out in Indonesia.
- An earthquake destroyed the Basilica of Assisi in Italy.
- Hurricane Paulina destroyed the temple of 'Baal-Christ' in Acapulco, Mexico.
- Princess Diana (representing the crown of England) was killed.
- Mother Theresa, advocate of exalting the Virgin Mary as co-redemptrix and mediatrix, died in India.

The claims and conclusions are breath-takingly imaginative, especially as some of the events took place *before* the prayer journey commenced. A 'significant prophecy' later revealed that the prayer teams to Nepal 'were up against a dragon [confirmed], that their prayer assault was sending arrows into the dragon which were causing mortal wounds'.

This kind of sensationalism is on the increase among many Christians, and is sweeping a lot of excitable people along with it. It has to be admitted that this wing of the church is where much of the action is today. This is no surprise, as everyone loves a sensation and the drama gives a great sense of momentum and achievement.

Before I move on to other examples, let me outline briefly why I believe this sort of sensation is not only unnecessary but in the long run is actively damaging to the Christian faith.

Most notably, the whole exercise and its remarkable conclusions make no claim to be based on biblical evidence. The impetus for the Everest expedition came from a personal conviction of the leader of one of the teams. The writer of the expedition report states that 'while in prayer the Holy Spirit clearly showed her' that Mount Everest was a principal stronghold of Satan over the most unreached parts of the world, and the seat of the Queen of Heaven. This is dramatic stuff. But how far can anyone trust a personal spiritual conviction to be true, in which no clear biblical revelation was involved? And how much is it likely to be the fruit of a fertile imagination?

The Christian faith only stands on a solid foundation in as far as it is an expression of truth. Every world religion and philosophy uses imagination and fantasy in its search for God, but Christianity is a faith that depends in its search on revelation. The advocates of the kind of spiritual exercise described here themselves admit that there is little teaching or example in Scripture either for their general practice or for their specific conclusions.

The Bible lays down principles for behaviour and practice, and presents a world-view both of the visible and the invisible world. Within those revealed parameters we may find the truth. In the practices of Operation Ice Palace, with its world-view of Satan seated on the slopes of Mount Everest as the Queen of Heaven, ruling the powers of darkness across Asia, we have an imaginative but unbiblical world-view of the devil and his powers. The team's deductions – that their prayers were in some way responsible for, or connected with, the deaths of Princess Diana and Mother Theresa (both events that took place before the Everest expedition) – are no less far fetched. They have lost touch with reality and hover on the lunatic fringe.

Discerning the bizarre

New Testament Christianity, even though full of strange and remarkable events, is amazingly free of the absurd and the bizarre. A blind man is healed, Jesus feeds 5,000 people with two loaves of bread and two fish, he walks on water, he casts out a demon from a demented boy. These are all strange and unusual things, but they are not bizarre, sensational or weird. Perhaps if Jesus had turned stones into bread, or had flung himself off the pinnacle of the temple, he could have been accused of sensationalism.

In the apocryphal gospels – those writings that were rejected by the early church as being imaginative and unreliable – there appear many examples of the kind of sensationalism that is notably absent in the true accounts of Jesus and the early church.

The *First Gospel of the Infancy of Jesus Christ* is one such apocryphal writing, produced by a Gnostic sect in the second century. It contains a strange mixture of fact and fantasy. Here we read that Mary, the mother of Jesus, gave his swaddling clothes to the three wise men, who threw them into the fire and were amazed when they were not burned. The gospel recounts the fanciful tale of the baby Jesus, while still in his mother's arms, prophesying about two thieves, Titus and Dumachus, whom they met on their way to Egypt, that they would 'be with me at the same time upon the cross'. There are stories of bewitched young men transformed into mules and miraculously restored to humanity when the virgin Mary sat upon them, and many more. Such stories are easy to dismiss as inventions and fables.

How should we respond, then, when we hear stories of amalgam tooth fillings being miraculously transformed into gold – no longer a second-century fantasy but a twenty-first-century 'miracle'?

> According to Christian internet sites and breathless press releases, dozens of charismatics in the south-east of England ... have been finding that they had miraculously acquired gold in their mouths or gold dust on their heads and hands while praying.[143]

So ran the press headline on 13 June 1999. The stories can be multiplied.

- Christians fall on their backs laughing uncontrollably, or barking like dogs – widely reported from many churches in what came to be known as the Toronto Blessing. Many were very excited. Many were very confused.
- Christians walk on water and climb trees like tree frogs, as reported by Mel Tari in his personal account of the Indonesian revival.[144] Water is turned into wine, the dead are raised and fire falls from heaven. Some of these phenomena were reportedly well documented.
- The Lord's Resistance Army in Southern Sudan is a fighting force led by Joseph Kony, 'a mad charismatic leader claiming to have religious powers'. It began when a Christian healer called Alice Lukwena led her supporters into battle against the Sudanese army 'with the promise that stones would be transformed into grenades in the name of the Holy Spirit'.[145]
- In two sensational and very popular books[146] Dr Rebecca Brown claimed extraordinary experiences as a converted Satanist, including face-to-face conversations with the devil and out-of-body travels around the world. She claimed that God sent an angel ('a shining white-robed figure ... with a drawn sword in his hand')[147] to kill her.
- In Civitavecchia, Italy, in 1995 a sixteen-inch-high statue of the Blessed Virgin Mary exudes a reddish fluid that appears to be blood from an area just below each eye. Such phenomena and other related appearances of the Virgin Mary are too numerous to mention.

It becomes imperative to distinguish between the imaginary and the real, the counterfeit and the true, the demonic and the truly godly. How can we tell the difference? For every genuine demonstration of God's miraculous power, there appears to be a sensational imitation – and God's people seem to be mesmerized by the extraordinary and the bizarre. But all that glitters is certainly not gold, and it is not acceptable to swallow every exotic wonder as evidence of God. There has to be – and there is – a way to tell the difference.

It is not only Christians who claim miraculous phenomena

and apparitions of the unusual. Hindus claim the miracle of the stone idol Ganesh who drank milk in Delhi and then in many places across the world. Burmese Buddhists witnessed the 'miracle' of multi-coloured light-beams appearing from a Buddhist monastery in 1997. In 1996 in Bolton, England, a Mrs Patel had a dream after she had bought an aubergine from her local shop. On slicing the vegetable in half, she saw that the seeds were formed in the Muslim symbol *Ya-Allah*, meaning 'Allah exists'. The heading on a web page dedicated to the weird and the wonderful and entitled the Miracle Page, from which these examples come, reads: 'Those who search for signs will find them ...'[148]

If true Christianity is characterized by, or even requires the evidence of, these kinds of excursions into the paranormal and the bizarre, then I count myself an unbeliever. Every time I pick up a magazine and read of some new Christian claim to an unusual phenomenon, I cringe. It does nothing for my confidence in the gospel to be beset by another far-out 'miracle'. Increasingly, Christianity is being viewed as an eccentric outpost of people out of touch with reality and relevance.

The tests of truth

In 1958 J. I. Packer wrote a marvellous little book called *Fundamentalism and the Word of God*, in which he examined the fundamentals of evangelical Christianity in contrast to the teachings of liberal theology. In those days Liberalism was a powerful force in the church and the Evangelicals struggled to compete with anything like academic credibility. Packer made an outstanding contribution in defence of the truth, and some things he said are relevant to our discussion in this chapter.

Among other things, he defines the liberal theological standpoint in these terms:

They accepted the viewpoint of the Romantic philosophy of religion set out by Schleiermacher – namely that the real subject-matter of theology is not divinely revealed truths, but human religious experience.[149]

This definition helps me. It helps me to understand that what we face today in the church is an onslaught of a new kind of liberalism – a theology whose real subject-matter is no longer divinely revealed truth (the evangelical truth of the Bible), but human religious experience ('what God is saying to me' and my feelings about him in the world today).

Packer calls it 'the problem of Authority', 'the most fundamental problem that the Christian church ever faces. This is because Christianity is built on truth: that is to say, on the content of a divine revelation.'[150]

When the so-called Toronto Blessing hit the churches in Canada, Britain and other places in 1994, many Christians were caught unawares, uncertain how to respond to these apparently supernatural phenomena. I was also intrigued by the movement, though I could never quite abandon my doubts and questions. But I wanted to believe the best and went along to several meetings, convinced that if there was blessing to be had, I wanted it. I was as sincere as I knew how to be. I relate more of these experiences in a later chapter, so I will not go into details here. What is relevant now is the way I, and the Christian public in general, responded to the Toronto phenomena. Together with a lot of people, I asked all the wrong questions:

- Is it spontaneous and divinely induced?
- Does it bear the marks of a true revival? How does it compare with the revivals of Jonathan Edwards?
- Does it make people hungrier for God? Does it give people a closer walk with God?
- Does it make people more eager to read their Bibles?
- Does it help people to resolve their problems? confess their sins?
- Does it make people more loving? nicer? easier to live with?

The list of questions grew long, but most of them were related to the experience, and the bottom line was: *Does it work?* If it worked, then it was seen to be good. If it didn't work, then it was suspect. But few people asked the right question until David Pawson wrote a book entitled *Is the Blessing Biblical?*[151] Pawson was right. It matters little what experience people receive, or what results ensue. What matters is whether it is true. Does it line up with the truth that God has revealed in his Word?

> A familiar educational principle states that if you can ask the right questions, you don't need the answers! I suppose it means that you are already thinking along the right lines and if you continue this course you will arrive at the right conclusions. In this book I have tried to ask the right questions.[152]

Jesus warned us many times to look out for the counterfeiters. 'For false Christs and false prophets will appear and perform great signs and miracles to deceive even the elect – if that were possible.'[153] Sadly, it appears to be very possible. If we are not asking the right questions, we will surely not get the right answers. If we are running after the sensational and the exciting, we will surely end up in a sensational crisis and an exciting mess, building our house upon a very dangerous quicksand and bringing our faith into public discredit.

12

An Unfair World
Is God biased?

Life is desperately unfair. No two people are ever treated equally. One person is born with a congenital heart disease, and another is born with a silver spoon in his mouth. One person is born to an alcoholic father and a prostitute mother and grows up in the streets, and another is born to nobility and riches. Why?

The World Health Organization reported that babies born in the United Kingdom in 1999 could expect 71.7 years of healthy life. The Japanese can expect to live three years longer than the British – 74.5 years. Too bad if you were born in Africa. Five African nations lie at the bottom of the list. If you were born in Botswana, Zambia, Malawi or Niger you will probably only live to about the age of 30. At the very bottom is Sierra Leone, where average life expectancy is only 25.9 years.[154]

The film *The Elephant Man* illustrates a tragic point. Why was Joseph Merrick so hideously deformed by large tumorous growths on his head that he joined a circus and became a freak attraction? Why did Helen Keller become blind and deaf at the age of two? And what of those horrific news reports of mentally retarded children locked away in institutions in Romania and Moldova? Why is the world such a cruel place and so unfair to so many?

The Bible records that Jesus faced the same questions, and he gave us no clear answers:

Now there were some present at that time who told Jesus about the Galileans whose blood Pilate had mixed with their sacrifices. Jesus answered, 'Do you think that these Galileans were worse sinners than all the other Galileans because they suffered this way? I tell you, no!... Or those eighteen who died when the tower in Siloam fell on them – do you think they were more guilty than all the others living in Jerusalem? I tell you, no!'[155]

I read somewhere that if you have a roof over your head, clothing on your back, the prospect of two or three meals a day and some form of transport, you are among the top fifteen per cent of the world's privileged. If you have two cars you join the top five per cent.

If there is anything that should make us question the righteousness of God, it is the unfairness of life. The fact that some are privileged because they were born in the right place at the right time, and others are doomed to misery because of the whim of fate, should make us all angry. It certainly raises some important questions about the goodness of God.

A few years ago I was invited to take a series of Bible studies with some Bangladeshi families who are involved in Christian ministry, and I prepared diligently a series of talks on the subject of love. It was a great subject, they were good talks and I had been blessed by the preparation. I still have the notes and I have repeated the series on other occasions.

My series began with the theme 'God is Love' from 1 John. I traced the nature of love and the difficulty John had – and we all should have – in believing that we are worth loving. Then I looked at the big question: Why does God love us?

- Is it because we look beautiful? No.
- Is it because we behave well? We don't.
- Is it because we flatter him or compliment him – or because we worship him? No.
- Is it because we improve his self-esteem – giving him glory? No.

Then why does he love us? Of course, the answer is that he loves us because he is Love – it is his nature to love, love is the quality of his being.[156] It should not surprise us that God loves us because his reasons for loving are not to be found in us, but in himself.

I was meditating on this message as I drove a minibus full of Bangladeshis out of Dhaka and up towards the beautiful tea gardens in Sylhet in the north-east of the country, where our retreat was to be held.

At midday we stopped in a small town for lunch, and after we had eaten I returned to the vehicle and was sitting in the driver's seat waiting for the others. A beggar lady came to my window to ask for money. I can't remember whether I gave her something – begging is very common and sometimes I give, sometimes I don't; it usually depends on the appearance of the beggar. If they are obviously thin, deformed or exceptionally ragged I tend to be more generous. This woman was probably aged about thirty and obviously poor. Two or three small children were hanging onto her sari. I probably gave her a *taka* or two.

She went off across the street and stood under a tree. I watched her as she pulled out her day's takings and started to count what she had. It was probably not more than twenty or thirty *taka* – equivalent to less than fifty pence.

And then it struck me – a thought that has haunted me ever since. God is love – he loves us because he is love. It is his nature to love. That means he loves everyone, regardless of whether they are good-looking or ugly, rich or poor, good or evil, privileged or underdog. That is the nature of his undeserved, unprejudiced love for his creation. That means that he loves that beggar woman as much as he loves me – no more, no less.

Why then is life so unfair? Why was I born to a relatively wealthy family in a country that has provided me with a good standard of living, education and the opportunity to hear about Jesus Christ and attend a loving church fellowship? And this woman was born in poverty, with no natural privileges and the obligation to beg for her meagre survival and that of her children. She never had the opportunity to learn to read or write and she almost certainly had never heard the gospel of Jesus Christ explained to her or attended a loving fellowship of believers. And yet God loves her as much as he loves me?

If God only loved those who loved him, that would not be a problem. If God had told us that he was selective in whom he chose to love, I could understand it. If God was prejudiced and partial, or a racist, it would make sense. If God was not good, or if he was weak and powerless, I could understand. But God has the power and the ability to do as he pleases. He has told us that he is love and he does not want any to perish. That lands us with a huge problem.

It raises further difficulties with my appreciation of the church. I hear about churches that spend millions of dollars or pounds on themselves, building crystal cathedrals and taking expensive holidays. I spend as much on a daily newspaper in my home country as that lady receives from her begging in a day. And yet the Bible tells me that God has poured his love into our hearts by the Holy Spirit.

Since that day I have lived with a certain sense of responsibility (sometimes akin to guilt) hanging over me, not to mention a huge question mark over the nature of God and his relationship to his world. I cannot understand why the church continues to be blessed, to sing happy songs and to enjoy the presence of God, while the world is so unfair and so unequal. How can so many of us Christians continue to remain in our protected enclave? The sums no longer add up.

A recent issue of *Time* magazine[157] contained the following facts and figures:

- There are an estimated 600 million children in the world living in poverty on incomes of less than $1 a day. That number has grown by 50 million in the last decade.
- In 44 countries of the world at least a third of the children under the age of 5 suffer from growth disorders due to malnutrition.
- 30,500 boys and girls under the age of 5 die every day, mainly from preventable causes.

- 130 million children in the world do not go to school, usually because their families cannot afford to send them.
- 60 million children aged between 5 and 11 work in hazardous circumstances.
- 2 million children have been killed in armed conflicts in the last 10 years.

These statistics are so common and so accessible that they usually make no impact on us. It is only when we see a beggar lady with her children counting her precious few *taka*, that world statistics collide headlong with our comfortable theology.

There is a popular teaching today (with an accompanying range of beautiful choruses to sing) which assures us that we are *special* to God. It is absolutely true. God looks on each and every one of us and he loves us with everlasting love. He has chosen us and we are special in his eyes.

But, however special I know I am to him, I am no more special, no more beloved, than the Bangladeshi beggar or the most tragic AIDS victim in Africa.

How are we supposed to answer this kind of dilemma? Or should we shrug our shoulders and consign it to the great mystery of life that has no answer? Life is complicated enough without bothering about the poor and the starving millions of Asia. And yet for the sake of integrity we must search for some solutions. In my mind's eye, God's reputation as a God of love is at stake. Does he care for his world? Or does he only care for the privileged? It is important to know.

I can only hazard some answers. I am still struggling to come to terms with the problem.

The facts of life

Jesus told his disciples, 'The poor you will always have with you.'[158] When we view this passage in its context, we see that Jesus is actually answering the very problem we are facing. A woman had just poured the expensive contents of an alabaster flask of ointment onto his head, and his disciples had objected. 'Why this waste?' they protested. 'This perfume could have been sold at a high price and the money given to the poor.' My instincts sympathize with the disciples. But Jesus did not jump to the same conclusion.

In effect Jesus is telling his disciples that it is necessary to keep a balance. There are times when it is right to help the poor. There are times when there are other priorities. Material equality is important but not absolute.

Furthermore, Jesus is saying that life is never going to be fair. There will always be poor people, and for many reasons. However much generosity the rich indulge in, poverty will always be a factor of life. Nor will people ever be equally privileged. The world contains inequalities that can never be resolved, contradictions that can never be reconciled. One day things will be very different, but for the present the poor will always be with us.

That in no way implies that God does not love the underprivileged. Scripture makes it clear that, if anything, God is biased towards the poor. There are hundreds of scriptures that indicate that. In fact, in heaven we will find, to our great surprise, that the poor have been specially honoured:

> Blessed are you who are poor ...
> Blessed are you who hunger now ...
> Blessed are you who weep now ...[159]

It appears to be one of those assumptions that we make from our distorted perspective that poverty implies a lack of interest on the part of God. Yet the Bible makes it clear that God loves the poor in a special way and perhaps paves the path for them, in his own supreme and sovereign way, to ultimately be more privileged in eternity. I cannot pretend to understand what that might mean.

The catastrophe of the fall

We can never overestimate the extent and consequences of the fall in Genesis 3, for that is where we need to look for an understanding of the messy disaster-ridden world in which we live. When Adam and Eve shook their fists at God, they were cutting off from his blessing not only themselves, but also the wonderful world that God had prepared for them:

> Because you ... ate from the tree about which I commanded you, 'You must not eat of it,' cursed is the ground because of you.[160]

The whole of creation, says Paul, has been 'subjected to frustration' and is in 'bondage to decay'.[161] We should not be surprised if things go wrong and the world is full of suffering and sadness, for that is how Adam and his rebellious descendants have made it. Whatever the urge of our problem-ridden minds, we must be slow to blame God. Likewise, from our limited and inadequate perspective, let us beware of holding him responsible for not stepping back sooner into history to judge the wicked and destroy the corrupt.

The rebellion in the Garden – humanity's first war of independence – affected far more than Adam's close relationship with his Creator. It affected the status of his descendants. It affected their relationship to one another – hence the murder in chapter 4. It affected the earth all around them, and the weeds sprang up in testimony to the fact that nature had caught the disease and run out of control. Within another few chapters we find the greatest natural catastrophe of all time – the world-wide flood and the destruction of all living things. Did God love those who died? Of course he did! But every effect has a cause, and God allowed to happen what had to happen.

In the light of the Bible's interpretation of world history, we ought to be surprised that so much goes *right* and that there is so much *good* in the world, because the world is in the grip of the 'rulers ... the authorities ... the powers of this dark world and ... the spiritual forces of evil in the heavenly realms'.[162] That is how the Bible explains this mess, and it makes a lot of sense.

Should we really blame God?

It is ingrained in human nature to look for someone to blame. Instinct compels us to hit back when we are hurt. Sometimes we are right. People should be held to account. But often it is a way to transfer blame, and we do it quite unfairly because we do not have all the facts. We don't see the whole picture.

So it comes naturally to blame God for the tragedies of a fallen world. Millions have cursed God because they blame him for suffering and sorrow. Someone must be held to account, and who more obviously than the One who created the darkness?

Let us be careful how we tread, because as human beings with a very limited perspective we do not see the whole picture, nor do we have all the facts. Here we are looking into the mysteries of the invisible world without seeing more than a fraction of what is really going on. We cannot make sense of the horizon while walking through the fog.

For example, common sense tells me that darkness is dangerous and pain is unpleasant. However, the discerning eye can find beauty even in the darkest corners. Read the extraordinary testimony of pastor Richard Wurmbrand in which he tells of his fourteen years in the brutal prisons of Communist Romania. He tells of the beauty and the ecstasy he found even in the darkest moments:

> The prison years did not seem too long for me, for I discovered, alone in my cell, that beyond belief and love there is a delight in God: a deep and extraordinary ecstasy of happiness that is like nothing in this world. And when I came out of jail I was like someone who comes down from a mountain top where he has seen for miles around the peace and beauty of the countryside, and now returns to the plain.[163]

We can never see what mysterious things God may be doing through the suffering and pain. In fact the pinpricks of light shine that much brighter where the darkness is deepest. That is part of what it means to discern spiritually things that logical thought would reject.

Sharing the pain

There is one further thing we have to cling to in the midst of all
the questions. It may seem like a contradiction in terms but it is
surely a key to understanding and certainly a key to survival:

> He was despised and rejected by men,
>   a man of sorrows, and familiar with suffering.
> Like one from whom men hide their faces
>   He was despised, and we esteemed him not.[164]

> When they hurled their insults at him, he did not retaliate;
> when he suffered, he made no threats. Instead he entrusted
> himself to him who judges justly.[165]

> This is how we know what love is: Jesus Christ laid down his
> life for us.[166]

A God who stood outside his creation, directing its affairs and
deciding its fate, would be fair game for accusation, but the
Christian God has himself plunged into the maelstrom of
human suffering and failure, wading through the sewage to
experience the horror and involve himself in the rescue operation. Like the firemen who streamed into the burning World
Trade Center on 11 September 2001, God involved himself in
putting out the blaze and risked perishing in the process.

The mystery of a God who himself chose to suffer – to
identify himself with his suffering creation – has been the subject
of theological fascination and enquiry for many centuries, and it
lies at the heart of uniquely Christian theology. The passion of
Christ was the awesome event that made the experience of
suffering – including injustice and inequality, squalid poverty
and criminal accusation – part of the experience of the world's
Creator. That is what makes it impossible for us to accuse God
of indifference or neglect. He has in suffering made himself one
with human sorrow. We can no longer point an accusing finger.

If we cannot understand how that makes sense of a rotten and
suffering world, then we need to cling to it anyway. It is a
mistake to go looking for scapegoats; instead we should try to

grasp the whole picture. That picture will only be fully available when history has been wrapped up and we can see it all from the perspective of eternity.

One further thing. It is usually those who hold onto the tiny light they have, who shed the most light for those around them. Those who curse the light find themselves in ever deeper darkness.

God has given us a job to do

We should also remember that, in the meantime, God has given us a job to do. It may look like an impossible job. It may look as though he has gone away into a far country, and will one day come back unannounced, angry with us for our failure. But the fact is that Jesus prayed to the Father in the upper room: 'As you sent me into the world, I have sent them into the world,'[167] and he followed up his prayer with the instruction: 'As the Father has sent me, I am sending you.'[168]

He followed his transfer of responsibility with the promise of power. Immediately after delivering the charge to his disciples, he gave them this pledge: 'Receive the Holy Spirit.'[169] And then he 'poured out his love into our hearts by the Holy Spirit whom he has given us'.[170]

God surely does love the Bangladeshi beggar – and the drug-destroyed prostitute in our back streets, and the condemned prisoner in a Thai jail – no less (and no more) than you or me. But he has said to you and me, 'Go and share your bread with them.'

Love that will not let me go

Whatever happened to the love that we are supposed to have in our hearts? According to Jesus that love is the hallmark of a Christian. This is how the world should recognize that we are his disciples, 'if you love one another'.[171]

It should be no surprise to us that Jesus made love so prominent in his final instructions to his followers. His Father was counting on them to restore love to an embittered and fractured world, to heal the wounded and restore the hurting, to lift up the downtrodden and to preach good news to the lost. And the New Testament church did well – not only preaching the gospel till their hearts burst, but healing the sick and distributing their goods to any who had need.

The church throughout history has not done so well, being often marked by arrogance and conflict, extravagance and greed. But in the midst of all the failures, let us not forget the outstanding example set by many who have laid down their lives in an unmatched demonstration of love.

I will not forget my meeting with Mother Teresa in a refugee camp outside Calcutta in 1971. It was a hot and humid day, as most days are in Calcutta. The monsoon had arrived and a fine drizzle soaked the city. It was at the height of the civil war in East Pakistan and ten million refugees had fled into India. We were swept up in the crisis.

The report came in one wet morning that there was an emergency in a refugee camp just to the north of the city. All of life was an emergency during those days and this was nothing unusual, so we pulled ourselves together, got into our old van and drove out to find the camp. It was about an hour's drive. That was where we encountered Mother Teresa.

It was not really a refugee camp at all, just a patch of ground set aside by the government, on which someone had erected bamboo structures with some form of roofing. These stood like gaunt skeletons with no walls and floors of wet sand. The wind was driving the rain and making them totally ineffective as shelters against the awful weather. A mass of bedraggled humanity, exhausted from their trek across the border, stood shivering in the rain, clinging to their pathetic bundles of belongings. To one side lay a heap of rolls of black plastic sheeting.

In the midst of this devastation was Mother Teresa, a tiny figure in her familiar white sari with blue borders, totally in control and giving people their orders.

We spent the afternoon under her firm command, unrolling the black plastic and cutting it into sheets that could be wrapped around the bamboo frames and spread on the earthen floors to make some kind of shelter for the refugees. The rain beat down continuously. Two refugees had died of cholera and their bodies were also wrapped in black plastic.

When the light began to fade we prepared to return to Calcutta. Since I was driving a van, the small lady in a white sari asked if I would give her a lift into the city. As we drove we talked about the crisis, about the war next door and about Calcutta, the city she had made her home for most of her life. I asked her if she thought there was any hope for the city. 'Oh yes,' she said and her eyes lit up. 'Things are so much better than they were when I first came here forty years ago.'

One cannot deny that the world was a better, fairer, more equal place because of her example and devotion. Mother Teresa loved the beggar as much as she loved her sisters. That should be the norm, not the exception, among Christian people.

13

Does God Care?

Statistics to shame us

If God sometimes appears to be unfair because so many are rich and even more are poor, how much more problematic is the spiritual state of the world. I have been committed to missions for more than thirty years now. For about twenty-four of those years I was actually resident overseas, mostly in India and Pakistan. I have seen a lot of missions and missionaries from the inside.

I am not a statistician, but like everyone else I am bombarded with statistics. I think God was very wise when he punished David for taking a census of the people of Israel.[172] Though I am not clear about the reasons why this was such a sin in God's eyes, I am aware that statistics can be used for many different purposes, and can also be distorted and made to mean almost whatever we please.

In 1978 the US Center for World Missions produced some publicity with the title *Penetrating the Last Frontiers*. It was accompanied by charts and diagrams and endless statistics. It sounded immensely impressive and generated a lot of excitement, which is of course what it was supposed to do, and that in itself was good. Suddenly the task of world evangelization seemed to be just around the corner. The US Center had discovered a way of presenting the goals to make them seem attainable.

However, reading the small print even in this optimistic

document revealed that 57% of the world's peoples 'still have no church or significant mission work reaching out to them ... they are simply not realistic candidates for membership in existing Christian churches'.[173]

Since that 'optimistic' projection was published, the world has grown in total numbers by a further two billion people.[174] I realize that already the figures are so large and meaningless that they have become unimpressive. The mind, mercifully, cannot take it in.

When I went to India in 1967 the task was impossible. There were 450 million Indians, most of them unreached and many of them unreachable. We were full of faith and distributed tracts with great zeal, convinced that it would make a difference. And indeed it did – in the lives of a few.

Official figures confirm that on 11 May 2000 the population of India reached 1,000 million, 'with a girl born in New Delhi the symbolic billionth citizen'.[175] In other words, in my active ministry lifetime, the population of India has more than doubled. That does not mean that 500 million have been added. It means that about 800 million have been added and 300 million have died and gone for ever. The figures are approximate and the mind boggles.

In percentage terms the statisticians say that the church is growing. In numerical terms there are more lost people in the world today than at any time before in history.

The incredibly extraordinary thing is that most of us don't really care.

I was always deeply moved by the story of Hudson Taylor, the great missionary pioneer who founded the China Inland Mission in the last century. He belonged to a previous generation and his vocabulary is now quaintly dated. He had been to China and returned to England for his furlough. During that time he wrote in his diary:

> Perishing China so filled my heart and mind that there was no rest by day and little sleep by night, till health broke down. I went to spend a few days in Brighton.

While he was there he attended a Christian service in the Pavilion.

> On Sunday June 25th 1865, unable to bear the sight of a
> congregation of a thousand or more Christian people rejoicing
> in their own security while millions were perishing for lack
> of knowledge, I wandered out on the sands alone, in great
> spiritual agony, and there the Lord conquered my unbelief
> and I surrendered myself to God for this service.[176]

It was the birth of a great mission to inland China that survives
today in the Overseas Missionary Fellowship. Sadly, few
Christians know the story of Hudson Taylor today and even
fewer are stirred, as he was stirred, by the fate of the lost.

*The most troubling problem here is the coldness and indifference in
my own heart. I know far too much to claim ignorance and yet
remain distressingly unstirred with passionate enthusiasm and zeal
for the gospel. I have no excuse. It is a disease that lies at the heart of
many Christians.*

*Worship and the enjoyment of God lie at the heart of true
Christian experience – but so do compassion and love for the needy
and the lost. So how is it that so many millions of wonderful
Christian believers can in practice be so self-indulgent and indifferent in their lifestyles?*

*We loudly deny the pluralist creed that there are many ways to
God. We protest when multi-faith services are held in our
cathedrals, because they appear to admit the equal validity of the
Hindu, Buddhist and Muslim religions to provide their adherents
with salvation. And yet in practice we ourselves are pluralist –
paying little heed to the fact that multi-millions across the world still
have never had their first chance to know Jesus Christ.*

When I was studying in Bible College and preparing to go to
India for the first time, I eagerly read the biographies of the
missionary giants of the last 200 years. I was touched by Hudson
Taylor, the five martyrs of the Ecuador jungle, John and Betty
Stam. I was fired by the dedication of C. T. Studd and his oft-
quoted challenge: 'If Jesus Christ be God and died for me, then
no sacrifice can be too great for me to make for Him.'

Then I travelled to India and found that missionaries were quite ordinary humans, who lived in decent houses, often much nicer than those of their national co-workers, and sometimes displayed very little zeal for evangelism. There are some outstanding exceptions. Over the years I have worked very closely with missionaries and have seen most of their strengths and weaknesses, and of course I am one of them – no better and no worse, with the same struggles and failures and human frailties.

I have met missionaries who cannot get along with their fellow missionaries. I have met missionaries who love to get away from the 'natives' and who speak badly about the country of their adoption. I have met those who have a love affair with their computers, or their accounts, or who have started up a business to get a visa and now spend most of their time trying to make their business profitable. Sometimes they call this 'tent-making'. I have met many who went home after a few years of frustration and failure, feeling disillusioned and defeated.

'Back at home' there is often huge indifference to what the missionaries are doing, and little understanding of or interest in the needs of the lost. In a volume of this size and nature I cannot begin to catalogue the weaknesses and the inadequacies of the missionary endeavour. Suffice it to say that it is often a far cry from the Acts of the Apostles and the missionary biographies of the nineteenth century – and there is a long, long way to go before the other half of the world hears the gospel.

My missionary heroes

So what is it that motivates me to keep going? Why do I feel that it is not all a hopeless, lost cause? Why do I still believe (in spite of my distressing emotional indifference) that the missionary endeavour is at heart still the most important, most underrated and most urgent aspect of the church's task?

A few years ago I drove my daughter back to her university, and for an hour or two we talked about missions. She had attended a YWAM Discipleship Training School and spent several short-term periods working in Spain, Albania and Morocco. She was seriously praying about her future, and she asked me about life as a missionary. We talked about the ups and downs, the strengths and weaknesses of missions.

When we arrived at her college in Canterbury, she thanked me as she got out of the car. 'Dad,' she said, 'after talking to you I have decided I don't want to be a missionary.' Daughters have a special ability to cut their fathers down to size! I had spent a lot of time telling her of the follies and the failures of missions, and of my conviction that, without being ready for disappointment and hardship, she should not think of following in my footsteps. Much to her credit, that was not her final word on missions, and she remains today committed to the wider task of the church, and – who knows? – maybe one day she will sense the tug and launch out into the heartache and the blessing of missionary endeavour.

The picture is by no means all negative. I have a catalogue of missionary success stories and missionary heroes, whom I admire and wish to emulate. There is no doubt in my mind that some of the most extraordinary unsung heroes are to be found in the far-flung places, doing astonishing things for God.

Roland Williams of Calcutta

I think of Roland Williams, an elderly Welshman who, as far as I remember, worked under a Mission Society but operated totally independently. I came to know him when I lived for two years in Calcutta. He was utterly simple and unpretentious. There was no guile in him. He slept at that time in a church hall and kept his bedding and other meagre possessions under the stairs during the daytime. He owned almost nothing, yet every day he would buy a stack of *chappatis* (round, flat bread) and make his way down to Sealdah Railway Station where he would hand out the food – and maybe some gospel tracts – to the hordes of refugees from East Pakistan who crowded the railway platform.

Roland had not been back to Wales for many years and he had no desire to go. He called Calcutta his home – these were his people, this was his life. We once offered him a free ride back to Wales in one of our vehicles, and he smiled and said he would think about it, but he never went. I have heard that he died a few years ago and so has gone to his reward. No-one has written his biography. In worldly terms he was not successful and he never lived at the heart of a revival or a mass movement. In fact few people have ever heard of him, but I am sure his name is celebrated in heaven.

The Wilders of Faisalabad

One of the most gracious and effective missionary couples I have ever known is John and Dorothy Wilder, who served for many years with the Presbyterian Church (USA) in Pakistan. While Dorothy raised the family, looked after the home and oversaw the running of mission schools, John established the work of the Pakistan Bible Correspondence School in Faisalabad, one of the most effective outreaches to non-Christians in the country.

My wife and I owed a special debt to the Wilders. When we had just arrived in Pakistan in 1979, new and inexperienced, we ran into a fair amount of deserved criticism from other missionaries because of some of the things we attempted to do. Senior missionaries can be very cruel to zealous newcomers who go against established practice. But the Wilders were always gracious, helpful and kind, even when they did not fully agree with us. I owe them a colossal debt of gratitude and admiration.

After establishing the Bible Correspondence ministry, John started a recording studio preparing radio programmes and making music and teaching cassettes. And then, a great achievement and to his lasting credit, he handed them all over to capable national leaders whom he had chosen and trained, before his retirement. It was a remarkable career, and the Wilders were typical of a generation of Presbyterian missionaries who left a lasting mark on the church in Pakistan.

Mark Buntain of Calcutta

Mark Buntain of the Assemblies of God church in Calcutta was well known in mission circles. His widow, Huldah, continued to lead the church after her husband's death. I knew Mark in the seventies when I used to attend his church in Royd Street every Sunday evening. He had built up the congregation from nothing and when I lived in Calcutta it was a flourishing fellowship of several hundred, with numerous different language congregations and daughter churches. Every night church volunteers would prepare hundreds of *parathas* (greasy fried flat-bread) and curry, and at daybreak they would feed up to 2,000 of Calcutta's poor.

Mark Buntain lived a colourful life and left a deep impression on thousands of Calcutta's residents. I well remember the tears in his eyes when he said a public farewell to his daughter as she left for college in America. The tears in Mark's eyes were genuine. He was an emotional man and I saw those tears at other times too, as he pleaded with his people to get right with God, or as he prayed in the side annexe after a Sunday evening gospel appeal. Sincerity, commitment and compassion marked his life.

I could extend this list for many pages, but space forbids. I still love to read the biographies of great missionaries and great Christians, though I realize that most biographies give a distorted and often unrealistic picture of their subject. But, if ever I am discouraged about the missionary task of the church (which is quite often), I have only to think of the procession of remarkable and dedicated people it has been my privilege to come close to, and sometimes to work with, over the last thirty-five years. They are an illustration of the reality of the Holy Spirit, still motivating ordinary men and women to do the extraordinary.

And what of the task?

Without greater commitment, or an astonishing outpouring of the Holy Spirit, the task of world evangelization looks truly impossible. As reassurance that we are making progress, the experts continue to provide some wonderful statistics. The US Center for World Mission is now claiming that the percentage of Bible-believing Christians rose from 10% of the world's population in 1993 to 11% in 1997 – 645 million people. 'Evangelical believers are growing at a rate of three and one half times that of world population,' they report.[177] And there are some remarkable signs of divine intervention in lands such as Indonesia, China, Korea and parts of Latin America.

There is a crescendo of mission activity in certain parts of the church. The Koreans are sending missionaries in increasing numbers in a new wave of militancy that puts the tired Western churches to shame. The enthusiasm of the Brazilians is stimulating. People are turning to Christ in large numbers in some areas of the world. But the cruel fact remains that many millions of the world's peoples have still never heard the message of Christ, and are unlikely to in this generation. World population, which has passed six billion, is growing out of human control and the task is overwhelming.

But, while there remains a huge area of mystery in God's ways, we can draw reassurance from two great facts:

1. God is in charge

God has told us that he is patient and faithful, 'not wanting anyone to perish'.[178] We can hold on to that, even if we cannot understand it. That is faith. From our ant-sized perspective, let us be very cautious to pass judgment on the eternal God, or dare to presume what he is doing. One day, no doubt, we shall see in clear perspective and then we shall understand. On that day we shall think, 'How stupid that we were so blind and failed to see what God was doing! How silly not to have trusted him.' Only foolish people pass judgment on the world on the basis of a newspaper report or a television programme. How small-minded can we be?

2. I can handle my patch

God has not made any of us responsible for the whole world. He has made each of us responsible for a patch. For some the patch is very small, perhaps just our own neighbourhood, or our village. For others God has given a special burden or concern for a city, a country or a people group such as children or drug addicts, refugees or immigrants.

Jesus told a parable[179] about a man who went on a journey. He entrusted his property to his servants before he left, and to each he gave a different amount, to 'each according to his ability'. We sometimes read this parable as though the Master were giving us talents and abilities, but it reads much more logically if we understand that the Master is giving us each a piece of his property to look after according to our ability – to some a large piece, to some a small. And our responsibility is to invest and serve faithfully in the area he has given to us. Beware the neglect of our patch.

That is not to say that we should not have concern for a wider area or aspect of God's world. But our patch is our prime responsibility.

Remember the starfish

I frequently return to the story of the starfish to help cut my world down to size. You may have read this before, but it is worth repeating:

An old man, walking the beach at dawn, noticed a young man ahead of him picking up starfish and flinging them into the sea. Catching up with the youth, he asked what he was doing. The answer was that the stranded starfish would die if left until the morning sun.

'But the beach goes on for miles, and there are millions of starfish,' countered the old man. 'How can your effort make any difference?'

The young man looked at the starfish in his hand and then threw it to safety in the waves. 'It makes a difference to this one,' he said.

And what of the lost?

And what of the lost? The endless line stretches away into the distance. Some mission specialists and spokesmen have vaunted attractive slogans – 'A Church for Every People and the Gospel for Every Person'[180] – and working plans for the evangelization of the remaining billions, and these have stimulated and energized many churches into caring action.

Others have organized prayer journeys, in which thousands have travelled to needy lands and prayed for a spiritual breakthrough. I still find it difficult to accept the huge expense of such trips, which, if we were honest, are sometimes little more than glorified tourism. I question whether it is good value for money, especially as the Bible appears to indicate that the location of prayer makes little difference to its effectiveness. Having made that small complaint, however, one cannot deny that such endeavours have motivated many people and churches to take the missionary task seriously.

It would seem clear to my questioning mind that a church that is not taking its world-wide responsibility to heart can be compared to a person taking a cool shower while his house burns. Amy Carmichael's little tract, in which she portrays people making daisy chains under the trees while multitudes of blind people fall over the cliff edge a few yards away, still forcibly portrays an uncomfortable truth.[181]

Until the church grasps the fact that it will take great and costly sacrifices, the commitment of a much greater slice of the annual budget and a concerted focus of compassionate concern on the world-wide spread of the gospel, the task probably will not advance adequately. The world grows bigger by the day and a generation passes into eternity every decade. It is an awesome thought.

14

Signs and Wonders
Power for living?

I should start this chapter with a confession. I have always longed to believe in and experience signs and wonders. About thirty years ago I stood in front of the Brethren Assembly in Ranchi, North India, after returning from several weeks of evangelistic campaigning around Bihar State. I was asked to give a report.

We had had a good tour, had preached the gospel in hundreds of village bazaars and streets to many thousands of people. We had distributed and sold thousands of Gospels and other Scripture books. It had been in every sense a successful evangelistic campaign. Yet I knew inside that it had not been enough.

In one bazaar where I had preached the message from the back of our old truck and then launched myself into the crowd to sell the books, I had been approached by a middle-aged Hindu.

'Do you believe what you have been preaching?' he began.

'Yes, I do,' I replied.

'It says in the Gospel,' he continued, speaking fluent English, 'that if you drink any deadly thing, you will recover.[182] Do you believe that?' I saw that he was setting me a trap.

'I believe it,' I said, 'but you have to take it in context.'

Ignoring my excuse, he went on. 'If I give you poison, will you drink it?'

'Now just a minute . . .'

'If you drink a glass of poison and recover, I will believe the message you have been preaching.'

Where was the power? I thought. Why did Jesus have to say that? And why was our preaching so powerless when it came to a demonstration of the truth? Did I have the faith to believe that I could drink poison and not be affected, according to Jesus' words? Should I take such a step – would it be true faith?

I stood before the Ranchi Assembly and confessed my frustration. I read from 1 Thessalonians: 'Our gospel came to you not simply with words, but also with power, with the Holy Spirit and with deep conviction . . .'[183] Where is that power, I asked them, which the Bible promises and we know so little about? Where is the power to do miracles, the power that demonstrates that our gospel is true?

It is a confession of personal frustration and inadequacy, partly because I know the answer and still feel inadequate.

Authentic or artificial?

When the so-called Toronto Blessing arrived in Britain in the summer of 1995, stories were rife concerning this manifestation of the supernatural. Even the national press picked up that something unusual was going on. Starting from South Africa and moving rapidly to Toronto, Canada, and thence to Britain, unusual phenomena were appearing in growing numbers of churches – evidence, some people said, of a fresh outpouring of the Holy Spirit. Large numbers of people were falling to the ground when prayed for. Some appeared to be drunk and lay for hours on the floor enjoying the presence of God. Others were overtaken with fits of laughter or tears. *This is it*, I thought. Now I am going to experience the supernatural power of God in my life and it is going to be authentic.

I not only read the stories in the papers. I talked with a lot of people who had experienced the Blessing. A personal friend and respected Christian leader told me how during a prayer meeting he had suddenly found himself laid out flat on the floor laughing uncontrollably, together with other leaders from his church, with waves of hilarious and warm good feeling wafting through him for hours on end. It was contagious, he said. It was clear that God was in it.

My wife and I went to a meeting at a church close to Bromley where hundreds were coming each night to be touched by the Holy Spirit. We joined the queue outside waiting to enter the church and spoke with someone who had been coming night by night to experience what he compared to a glorious drunkenness as the Holy Spirit overwhelmed him.

Our hearts were full of faith and expectancy. At last God was going to meet with us. After a short introduction, we were invited to push back the chairs and stand waiting our turn, when teams of trained church members would come and pray for us. As we stood we watched as one after another fell on the ground, weeping or laughing or just lying around peacefully on the carpet. After an hour and a half we were tired of standing on our feet, and at last I was beckoned over to someone who was ready to pray for me.

I had observed that the praying teams never gave up on anyone until they were flat on the floor, so I knew what was expected. I closed my eyes and waited while a kind middle-aged gentleman began to pray for me. His prayer went on and on and I was still on my feet, waiting for the touch of God. Unable to keep him waiting for ever, and feeling a gentle reassuring hand on my back and a slight – ever so slight – pressure on my chest, I submitted to the inevitable and allowed the kind man and his assistants to lower me to the carpet, doing my best to make it look genuine. I lay there, exhausted after standing on my feet for so long, but fully aware that this was no supernatural experience, but an act of kind manipulation. It had little to do with the power of God and it left me more confused and increasingly sceptical.

How many others in that room had undergone a similar manipulation to myself? It is embarrassing, apart from the stigma it might attract, to be seen not to be responsive to what God appears to be doing.

It was not the end of our Toronto experiences. We went to the heart of the movement, Holy Trinity Church, Brompton, raised our hands and waited, but again were bypassed and disappointed. We were prayed for a number of other times and increasingly I was determined that, if I were to receive the blessing, I was going to be sure that it came from God and was not pressed upon me by some willing helper eager to push me down on the floor.

I suspect that my experience was not unusual during that long summer. Whatever the leaders of the movement told us from the platform, it was clear that in many churches spiritual people were expected to spend time on the floor and those who failed to do so were regarded as resisting the Holy Spirit. The teaching went around that God's special blessing was reserved for the horizontal – fervently denied from the platform, but asserted by the attitude of the faithful. This naturally provided a considerable incentive to get down on the carpet and hope to receive all that God wanted to give in the way of good feelings. It created a lot of phoney experiences in many churches.

So what is this power of God that is celebrated in the Bible and fills the pages of a range of popular Christian books on our shelves? Is it authentic? Or is it reserved for special people? Or is it just a psychological hoax that catches the gullible and the weak-willed?

Why are these demonstrations of the power of God so arbitrary and often meaningless? I would find it easier to understand if there was some pattern, some compassionate consideration, some moral purpose behind the demonstrations of power. If it were the poor who received 'miracle' gold teeth, or the terminally ill who always received the healings, or the front-line missionaries who in their desperation were filled with fresh power – that would make some sense. But so often it is the middle-class and well-heeled for whom the 'Blessing' adds further comforts to their already comfortable lifestyle. What does that say about the God who dispenses gifts so arbitrarily and meaninglessly?

Newsweek[184] magazine carried an article entitled *What Miracles Mean*, in which journalist Kenneth L. Woodward investigated miracles – 'extraordinary events that are the result of special acts of God'. But these 'acts of God' are not confined to Bible-believing Christians. 'Many Jews and Buddhists,' he says, 'as well as Christians, Hindus and Muslims, still look for – and, by their own accounts, experience – miraculous interventions in their lives.'

He then describes some of those miracles. Tyler Clarensau, a fifteen-year-old member of Park Crest Assembly of God Church in Springfield; USA, suffered for years from malformed knee joints that surgery had failed to correct. A group of teenagers prayed for his healing and Tyler was amazingly healed. 'He began to do deep knee bends, something he hadn't accomplished in years.'

In 1966 Angela Boudreaux was diagnosed with liver cancer and given two weeks to live. A loyal Roman Catholic, she prayed fervently to her favourite saint, Father Xavier Seelos, a priest whose bones lay buried in her parish church. Incredibly, the huge tumour in her liver began to shrink, and Mrs Boudreaux is alive and well, thirty-four years later.

There are testimonies of miracles from other religions too. Maharaj Krishna Rasgotra, a retired foreign secretary of India and devoted Hindu, suffered a heart attack in 1986 and received healing from his favourite guru, Satya Sai Baba. The mother of song-writer Shoshana Levin, a devout member of a Jewish Hassidic group in New York, was miraculously healed of stomach cancer in 1992 after receiving a blessing from her rabbi.

Is all this a demonstration of the power of God? Or the power of Satan? Christians often make stupendous claims about what God is doing in signs and miracles, but people from other faiths are no less zealous in claiming miracles as proof of God's blessing. So what do miracles demonstrate? Kenneth Woodward concludes his article with an old Hassidic saying: 'He who believes all these tales is a fool, but anyone who cannot believe them is a heretic.'

Two clear conclusions stand out from this confusion:

- Firstly, it is undeniable that miracles do happen. They happened in Jesus' day and they happen today – unusual phenomena that cannot be explained by the normal rules of scientific investigation.
- Secondly, miracles do not actually prove anything. Those who claim that unusual phenomena are a mark of some special divine blessing on their belief system are countered by those from other creeds who also experience miracles. Jesus said that God 'causes his sun to rise on the evil and the good, and sends rain on the righteous and the unrighteous'.[185] Only foolish people dare to make greater claims.

But Jesus promised power

The dilemma remains. The life of Jesus was replete with unusual phenomena – people were healed and rose from the dead, bread and fish multiplied and Jesus walked on water. The list is impressive and the Gospels indicate that each miracle was more significant than a mere spectacular intervention to meet a need. The apostle John uses the word 'Sign' to describe many of the miracles he records.

Like any signpost, the miracles in the Gospels are pointers to something significant. They indicate more than they demonstrate. They make no special claim to uniqueness, but they are there to underline and emphasize a truth: that this Jesus is the Son of God and his coming is with power.

Then Jesus promised that same power to his disciples. It was his last great promise to them, and it must likewise have had distinct meaning if Jesus was truly the unique Son of God. The experience of power is an essential element of true Christianity, and the promise was followed by an outbreak of unusual phenomena – tongues of fire, rushing wind, signs and wonders and healing miracles.

But what concerns us now is the place and purpose of that power for today.

'You will receive power when the Holy Spirit comes on you,' said Jesus just before he was taken up into heaven,[186] *and 'many wonders and miraculous signs were done by the apostles.'*[187] *Is that therefore the normal Christian life? Or was it reserved as a sign of the birth of the church? Or is it only for exceptional saints and emotional churches? Or should it be my regular and normal Christian experience? If so, what is wrong with me?*

I have a space on my bookshelves that I reserve for risqué books – 'to be treated with caution'. I would not call them all heresy, though some of them are both heretical and dangerous, and others hover on the borderlines. Nor would I call them all unbiblical, because some of them are full of Scripture and even pass the tests of broad evangelicalism. But there are a wide range of books, available in our Christian bookshops, that I believe need to be kept apart because they promote popular and dangerous distortions of the truth which are ultimately damaging to the many who love to read them.

On that shelf I keep the two most popular Christian novels of recent years, *This Present Darkness* and *Piercing the Darkness* by Frank Peretti. These are exciting stories brilliantly written and full of drama – the ingredients of a best-seller. They deserve to be popular. What they do not deserve is to be taken seriously. Sadly, many Christians take them much too seriously and have drawn their world-view from them and not from the Bible. On the whole Peretti's books are easier to read and often more exciting.

They portray a world which is in many respects like the world we live in, and then draw aside the veil to picture the parallel but normally invisible realm of the spirit. They tell an exciting tale of the interaction between these two worlds, and the result is a story of constant supernatural intervention and sensational power encounters. It is a world of make-believe, but it is presented as the real world – if we could only draw aside the veil and understand all that is going on.

There is surely some truth in Frank Peretti's thesis, and many Christians have had their prayer lives stimulated to a fresh sense of urgency by a vivid awakening to the supernatural dimension. Thus far his stories are valid. Peretti, however, has done a huge disservice to Christians by inviting us to believe that this is the normal Christian life – signs and wonders, power encounters, miraculous interventions, dramatic rescues and instant answers to prayer. To be honest, life just isn't like that.

That power is a promise for the believer is clear, but what does that promise mean? Is it the power to live in the miraculous, to live in daily expectation of the impossible? If not, then what is the power?

Power for every day?

There is no question that miracles and unusual phenomena do take place throughout the Bible, though not with even regularity. In the days of the Judges 'the word of the Lord was rare; there were not many visions',[188] and we must beware of getting a distorted impression. However, the Gospels and Acts are replete with 'signs and great miracles'. People are healed miraculously at a word from Jesus and his followers. The dead are raised. Water is turned to wine and a gold coin is retrieved from the mouth of a fish. Those things had their clear and meaningful place in the New Testament.

But are the events that surround the life of Jesus and the birth of the church an insight into life as it is ought to be lived through all the ages – 'normal' New Covenant experience? Luke wrote his two books – the Gospel and Acts – to describe a very unusual and utterly unique period of history, 'an account of the things that have been fulfilled among us'.[189] Why did Paul recommend to Timothy that he should 'stop drinking only water, and use a little wine because of your stomach and your frequent illnesses'?[190] Why didn't he command a miracle or recommend that he claim his healing? Peter and Paul were both miraculously delivered from prison once – but then Paul was imprisoned again. 'I am in chains,' he wrote to the Philippians.[191] And to Timothy: 'I am suffering even to the point of being chained like a criminal.'[192] Why did God not deliver him once again with a miracle? Was his imprisonment any less a sign of God's favour and power than his deliverance?

The miraculous healings and dramatic interventions are recounted, not to set a new standard of normality, but because they were so remarkable and exceptional. Books, magazine articles and newspapers are written today for the same reason – not to tell us what happens every day, but to tell us what has happened that is unusual and newsworthy. The miraculous had arrived in the lives of ordinary people – not as an everyday assumption, but as an everyday possibility.

As with many things in life, the truth surely lies between two extremes. There are those who say that miraculous events were exclusive to the first-century launch of the church and the miraculous has now been withdrawn from the church. That view is not as common nowadays as its opposite – that the Christian life should be lived in the supernatural realm, with the unexplainable established as part of everyday experience.

But where is the power today?

My mother was a hard-working widow with a chip on her shoulder. She had married in her mid-thirties and had five wonderful years with my father. He had won the Military Cross in the Great War for bravery under fire, and was very frustrated not to be able to go to the front lines when the 1939 war broke out.

Instead he was stuck in Jamaica as resident magistrate, and that was what he was doing when he was tragically killed in a car accident in 1943. He skidded off the road and overturned down an embankment. It was a bitter blow to mother. The war was still on, she was thousands of miles from her family and she had to cope with the grief on her own.

She had two small children on her hands, very little money and a long wait to get a safe passage back to England. She finally got a booking on the S.S. *Rimitaka* in 1945. My earliest memories are of the ship waiting for a convoy in New York harbour to escort us. There were still German U-boats in the Atlantic, but we arrived safely in Liverpool several weeks later. After more than five years away she expected a warm welcome from her mother. But the old lady was set in her ways. Instead of celebrating she sat down to a game of 'Halma' with my uncle – just as she had done every evening throughout the war. My mother was deeply hurt.

We moved into the top floor of my grandmother's large house, and my mother took a teaching job to keep food on the table. They were hard years and she became very bitter at the way life had treated her. But things only got worse.

My mother woke up one morning in 1950 with fits of shivering. The doctors diagnosed jaundice and a prolapsed uterus, and she went into hospital for an operation. Then they decided her real problem was polio. In the 1950s before the vaccine arrived, polio was a dreaded diagnosis that condemned thousands to lives on crutches and in wheelchairs.

> The hopeless despair of finding myself crippled, desperately poor, with no job and usually in pain made me even more resentful. One clergyman visited me and he was much too frightened to talk about religion ...[193]

Mother was a strong-willed woman and refused to give up easily. She managed to walk slowly for up to 100 yards at a time, though she had to wear a steel spinal support night and day, needed a walking-stick and had a spring in her shoe to help her lift her dragging foot. She had a wonderful physiotherapist called Mr Selmes who kept her going. Slowly she learned to drive a car again.

Medically there was nothing much more to be done for her. Apart from the physio she was doomed to live the rest of her life as a cripple. She packed my brother and me off to boarding-school as soon as we were old enough. She wrote:

> I do remember feeling sure that I wasn't meant to be crippled for the rest of my life, but I couldn't see a way out and every

visit to a new doctor or specialist returned the same answer: 'There is nothing more we can do.' My hopes would be raised and the negative answer dashed me to new and deeper despair. Even my beloved Mr Selmes told me he didn't think I would ever be any better.

She ordered a wheelchair and went through a bout of other sicknesses and intense pain, including gall-bladder problems that threatened another operation.

About this time she read a book on healing written by an old priest by the name of Father Jim Wilson (the brother of Edward Wilson, who died with Captain Scott in his ill-fated expedition to the Antarctic in 1912). Mother wrote to the author and they began to correspond.

She had her operation and got her wheelchair. On one level she was sinking ever deeper into despair. On another level, for the first time, through her correspondence with Jim Wilson, she began to believe that things could change.

We were at boarding-school throughout this period and only knew a fraction of what she was going through. I do, however, have a distinct memory of one Sunday in May 1956. For reasons I cannot explain, I knew that my mother was going to be healed. I didn't know why, but the memory of that conviction is still crystal clear in my mind.

Jim Wilson had been to visit her the previous week. It was all very simple. They had talked for a while and then he said, 'Think about Jesus,' and he put his hands on her and prayed for her. Let me tell the story in my mother's own words:

On Monday I stayed in bed most of the day ... On Tuesday Mr Selmes came for my treatment ... On Wednesday morning I did my exercises and found I could make movements I had not been able to make for six years. I crept out of bed and without my sticks I walked up and down the sitting room. Then I went upstairs without the sticks. I couldn't believe myself and I remember saying, 'This is different – this is real walking!' My heart was bursting. On Thursday I walked almost to town and on Friday a good mile and back.

On Sunday I went to church and was able to walk in. The verger who had helped to push me in my wheelchair the previous Sunday was speechless.

She went to her doctor and he was astounded. He said, 'Who has done this for you?' and confirmed that the nerve contact had been re-established. He advised her to take it gently, but mother was a very determined person. She wrote afterwards: 'In this he was wrong – quite wrong. I needed no slow muscular rehabilitation. I was alright straight away and had no stiffness or aching in my limbs at all.'

All that happened in 1956. It seems like a long time ago but is as fresh as yesterday. That summer we went to Austria for a summer holiday. We stayed at 6,000 feet and walked in the mountains for hours every day.

Mother was always careful to give the credit to the Lord. From that day to the day she died in 1977 she never looked back. She put away her sticks, sold her wheelchair and spent the rest of her life trying to help other people realize that no difficulty is too severe, no depression too deep, and with the help of God anything is possible.

Just the beginning

Mother's healing remains the most intimate demonstration of miraculous power I have experienced, but by no means the only one. I have known others who have been similarly healed or have witnessed otherwise unexplainable demonstrations of God's grace and power.

But I have to say that, marvellous and acceptable as such unusual phenomena are, they surely must remain secondary to, and are overshadowed by, the power of God in much more ordinary, everyday circumstances.

When the apostle Paul prayed for the Colossian Christians he asked God that they might be 'filled with the knowledge of his will' and that they might be 'strengthened with all power according to his glorious might'. And then he explained why he wanted them to have 'all power'. It was not for the working of great miracles or the demonstration of spectacular signs. It was 'for all endurance and patience with joy, giving thanks to the Father'.[194]

The apostle Paul realized that God's power was not demonstrated simply in the miraculous and the extraordinary, but was far more needed, and far more visible, in the everyday, to see his people through difficulty, temptation and trial. Perhaps God's power was more in evidence in Paul's imprisonments than in his deliverances.

Power in a broken body

I remember visiting a young woman in hospital when I was for a short time a student in Switzerland. I do not remember her name and cannot name her illness, but I can never forget her face. She was lying in bed almost immobilized by a large lung machine to which she was attached and which was her life support. To all outward appearances she had no quality of life and no hope of improvement. But her face shone and she exuded only gratitude and happiness. Meeting her was memorable and illustrated the amazing power of God in a broken body.

Power in suffering

Nor can I ever forget listening to Richard Wurmbrand, author of the best-selling *Tortured for Christ*[195] and many other books. Pastor Wurmbrand had spent fourteen years in prison in Communist Romania for his faith, before being released and shortly afterwards exiled to the West. Of all the people I have ever met, he probably knew more about the power of God for endurance with joy than any other. He came to our Bible college to visit one of our lecturers, H. L. Ellison, who as a CMS missionary had baptized him before the war. Pastor Wurmbrand spoke to the student body. His appearance was still worn and haggard and his sunken eyes had dark rims around them, and yet his face glowed as he described the experiences of his imprisonment and the joy of suffering for Christ. How can one explain such happiness in the midst of the most horrendous extremities of human degradation?

Power in resisting temptation

I have a Pakistani friend who works in a government department in Lahore. His pay, like many salaries in government positions, is quite inadequate to sustain a reasonable standard of living, and most employees accept that they need to look for other ways to supplement their income. There are many ways to do this, but the easiest and most obvious is to look for, and manipulate, payment for unauthorized services – in other words, to take bribes. Sadly, that is how many people survive in that society. My friend had as many opportunities to improve his income as anyone else in the office, but he refused to take them. He believed that bribery was wrong. His fellow workers considered him strange and stupid, but he stuck to his godly principles, and lived at a simpler level, within his meagre income. That, to me, demonstrates the power of God more than a display of supernatural pyrotechnics.

Power to live for Christ

Aslam Khan was converted from Islam to Christ in 1927 in Pakistan, as a result of which he was rejected by his family and for many years had no contact with them. I only came to know him when I arrived in Pakistan in 1979, by which time he was in his senior years and a highly respected Presbyterian pastor. He had bushy eyebrows and piercing eyes, which he would focus with extraordinary intensity when he felt passionately about something. He was especially passionate about his own people –

not just his family in Gujrat district, but the whole Muslim community, and he had dedicated his life to bringing people to Christ. This was no two-week wonder with a bubbling testimony of the miraculous, but a man of God who had walked with Christ for more than fifty years through many sorrows and hardships. Aslam Khan was, for me, an outstanding illustration of what the apostle Paul calls 'this treasure in jars of clay to show that this all-surpassing power is from God and not from us'.[196] In his latter years his family welcomed him back and he spent some of his last years with them in their village home, accepted by them and able to talk freely with them about Christ.

So, am I still frustrated by the lack of power in my life? Yes, I am, and I expect I always shall be. It will remain for ever unclear to me why the promise of power is so clear in Scripture and sometimes so hard to discern in my own life. But is this frustration going to cause me to deny the reality of God's power or the reliability of his promise? No, I have witnessed too much, experienced too much, understood too much ever to be able to deny that God's power is present and available. And I know enough to be sure that we are often looking in the wrong direction while God's power is at work, and so we miss its greatest evidence.

15

Unanswered Prayer
The indifference of God

I had worked in Calcutta in eastern India for two or three years and knew the city well. When the OM ship *Logos* was due to pay her second visit to Calcutta I was asked to do the advance preparation. This was in May 1973 and it generated a lot of excitement in the churches. I worked hard, gaining the formal local government permissions, arranging matters with the shipping agent, and designing a programme and publicity for conferences and other on-board events.

The ship was due to be berthed at the Man-of-War Jetty, a very suitable location where small ships could dock in the Hooghly River and be easily accessible for the general public. As a complement to the ship's facilities, we borrowed a large marquee from the Assemblies of God Church and erected it beside the pier. It had been used in years gone by for the first meetings of the church before they built their beautiful facility on Royd Street. We organized a coffee bar in the tent for the general public as an opportunity to relax and talk with local Christians.

And then we planned the highlight of the ship's visit, to take place shortly before her departure. This was to be a public concert held on the open grassy area close to the tent. We called it the Joy Festival, and we invited several of the main local Christian choirs to participate. Before the ship's arrival we held a whole night of prayer for the city and especially for blessing on the ministry of the *Logos*.

The ship arrived and the programme ran well. Thousands came to visit and press publicity was good. As the principal organizer I was physically and emotionally fully involved. The big night – the Joy Festival – was approaching, and the arrangements were working well, with the ship's music director, Frank Fortunato, taking control. The event was bathed in prayer and we had high expectations. On the day of the concert a platform was erected near the quayside, and several hundred chairs were hired. A borrowed piano arrived and stood on the platform. It promised to be a great evening.

I remember coming out of the ship half an hour before the concert was due to begin. People were beginning to arrive. The AoG choir drove up in their school bus, and the Youth for Christ group was also there. Frank Fortunato was on the platform warming up on the piano. I was so thankful to God that I was part of such an event.

And then I felt the wind.

There is a certain cold wind that occasionally blows down the Hooghly River, and it always spells trouble. I had felt it before and I knew what it meant. Rain.

I ran to the stage and grabbed Frank. 'Let's pray,' I said, and we huddled together at the side of the platform and prayed our hearts out for a miracle. It was ten minutes to seven, and we cried out to God. My memory flashed back to the incident in Watchman Nee's book *Sit Walk Stand* when he prayed for rain on a specific day and it poured down just as he had requested.[197] 'Where is the God of Elijah?' Could that same God not stop the rain that now threatened? It made no difference. Frank went back on stage and started to play a few defiant chords of faith on the piano. It seemed quite pathetic at the time, like King Canute trying to turn back the waves. Just on the stroke of seven o'clock the heavens opened and for the next half hour the rain poured down.

I don't know what happened to the choirs. By the time it was over they, and their bus, had disappeared. A lot of people, including myself, ran for the tent and huddled beneath it, though it provided little real shelter and some sensible people tried to urge us outside in case it should collapse under the weight of the water.

It was all over in thirty minutes, but the scene was one of devastation. The piano was soaked through to its strings. The site of our Joy Festival was water-logged, a lake standing inches deep. The tent was sagging and torn – it never recovered and was later disposed of. That was the climax of our programme in Calcutta and a few days later the ship sailed away.

But no less than the concert, my faith was pitched into a new crisis. Images flashed into my mind of my heavenly Father, seeing me wearying myself to please him, ignoring my cries for help and stamping (maybe even with some malicious sense of satisfaction) on the pride of my offering to him. Didn't he treat Job a little bit like that? 'Let's see what we can do to make life hard for him. See if he can pass the test.'

Unanswered prayer

'Teach me the patience of unanswered prayer.' So runs the line of a familiar hymn, but what sort of theology is that? 'Imitate those who through faith and patience inherit what has been promised,' says the writer to the Hebrews.[198]

There is no believer under the sun who has not discovered that God sometimes does not answer prayer, whatever his promises may say. 'I will do whatever you ask in my name,' says Jesus. 'You may ask me for anything in my name, and I will do it.'[199] Whatever did he mean?

Some super-spiritual triumphalist with all the answers will always come along with a cliché to the effect that we only need to know his will, or claim the promise with sufficient faith and expectation, or some other similar condition, and the answer will be automatic. The name-it-and-claim-it teachers have watertight answers to these difficulties. Here is one of Kenneth Copeland's golden keys:

The only people who pray 'if it be Thy will' are those who don't have any hope or expectancy. If you've been praying that way, stop it! Go to the Word and find out what God's will is. The Word of God *is* His will. It *is* His will for you to be well. It *is* His will for you to be prosperous. It *is* His will for you to lay hands on the sick and it *is* His will for them to recover.[200]

Did Jesus not pray, 'Not as I will but as you will'[201] in the Garden of Gethsemane? And is God's will really so obvious? Copeland's wife Gloria holds out some other appealing conditions:

It is God's will for you to be healed, but your faith cannot operate beyond your knowledge of God's Word ... Healing is always available to the believer, but faith has to be released in order for you to receive the healing power of God ... Believe you receive your healing when you pray, not when you feel better. This is how faith works ... All you have to do is expect to receive. Expect to receive. Expect God to bring healing into your body.[202]

Here is T. L. Osborn's simple formula:

Any person can turn any promise of God into the power of God equal to what it promises by believing that promise enough to act upon it.[203]

To be honest, such teaching holds a simple logic, which is very appealing. But it invariably results in one of several inevitable outcomes.

- Either it loads the blame on us for having insufficient faith if and when we do not receive instant results – for not knowing his will, or having inadequate hope and anticipation, or failing in some other vital condition – and we end up under terrible condemnation for failure.
- Or we land ourselves in cruel hypocrisy and denial, clinging to unreality and pretending that God has done something he hasn't. Numerous are the tales of people who have 'claimed

their healing' from God, yet they limp about the world convinced that their headache, or their cancer, or their disease, is healed. They fool no-one but themselves.

- Or we give up, on the reasonable assumption that God doesn't keep his Word – it just doesn't work. This is perhaps the saddest consequence of all, because at this point faith and hope die together.

Some Christians are satisfied with the easy cliché: 'God answers every prayer with a Yes, a No, or a Wait.' That has given me small satisfaction. As the wind was whistling down the Hooghly River, and I pleaded with God to stop the rain, there was no time for waiting. The answer had to be Yes or No. In that instance it was clearly No.

As I revised this chapter I received an urgent request for prayer for a young missionary family. The husband had been taken ill with a mystery parasite and the doctors gave him two months to live, barring a miracle. This was what he wrote:

> I feel like I am in a very dark valley right now. I have been praying for so long for help with no response, that I have become discouraged in prayer ... My prayers now are very elemental, 'Father, save me!' But the pain continues each day and I continue to lose weight. Please pray not only for my body, but for my spirit. I have not known fear like this before.

Easy clichés and neat theological explanations make little impression in such times of urgent need. When your friend is dying of a mystery illness and you are praying for healing, there is slim comfort in thinking that God might say 'Wait'. The answer must be 'Yes' or 'No'. And it is hard to accept that a God of love might say 'No'.

I had another such friend, an active Christian leader in Pakistan with an outstanding ministry. His leukaemia was diagnosed in August. In September he was admitted to hospital. Many Christians prayed urgently for his healing and were sure that God was doing a miracle. In October he died. It was a devastating blow for many who had prayed with urgent faith.

It is a mystery, which sometimes shakes and sometimes shatters faith. And sometimes faith is strengthened.

Answered prayer

It is no less a mystery when God does answer prayer.

It was a hot and heavy July day when I was invited to take a meeting in a Punjabi village outside Lahore. My friend and translator, Javed, knew the community well and had arranged the meeting. Like many such occasions, no preparations were made until we had actually arrived in the semi-darkness. Then we had to take tea before anyone began to settle down for the service.

I was not in a good mood and wanted the evening to pass by quickly. For one thing, it was hot, extremely hot, and there was not a whisper of wind. The meeting was held outside and there was no electricity for lights or fans. Then one of the local people decided I needed cool air, and started to wave a hand-held fan about six inches from my face as I was trying to preach. It irritated me endlessly. By the time I had finished my sermon, it was late and my faith was at an all-time low, and I wanted to get home to bed. But before I could get away I had to pray for the sick. As is traditional, a line of people waited to get a special prayer for their ailments.

I had noticed at some distance an old lady lying on a string bed. She was clearly very old, quite sick and probably ready to go to her Maker, but I was called over to pray for her healing. I did as I was instructed, but I had little faith that anything would happen.

The next morning, so Javed told me afterwards, the old lady was first off her bed, making food for the rest of the household. Her healing was absolute, and not only that, but the local Muslim priest had watched us as we prayed for her. Over his mosque loudspeaker the following Friday he announced that 'These Christians pray that the sick will be healed, and they are!' She lived for another three months, but her healing on that night was without question.

The enigma of the mind of God

I confess that prayer remains a deep mystery to me. Of some things there is no doubt at all – that it is important to pray, that God listens to those who speak to him and that he cares for his people's welfare. God is no slot machine – drop in your coin and the answer falls into the tray – but nor is he indifferent. Why he makes such great promises to those who come to him in Jesus' name remains one of the great adventures of our relationship with him.

Pray anyway!

It is clear that we are commanded to pray, and to pray with faith that we will be heard. In a certain sense, the answer to our prayers is secondary to our perseverance. Jesus told a story about a widow who came to plead for justice from an unrighteous judge.[204] It is hard to equate God with the judge, 'who neither feared God nor cared about men'. But that is not the point. The lesson is given to teach us that we 'should always pray and not give up'. The fact that God is neither unrighteous nor unsympathetic should give us even greater incentive to keep going, even if we do not understand or see quick results. Prayer is a discipline as well as a privilege.

I find the story of Lazarus' death very helpful.[205] Lazarus was ill – very ill, and his sisters sent for Jesus, knowing that he, the miracle-worker, could heal their brother. John is very nonchalant in the way he tells the story. 'Jesus loved Martha and her sister and Lazarus. Yet when he heard that Lazarus was sick, he stayed where he was two more days.' That comes across as an insult. Though he loved them so much, he did nothing at all to help them in their hour of need. He waited till he was sure that Lazarus was beyond healing – and then he went.

Is it any surprise that both sisters were angry with him when he finally arrived? They complained, 'Lord ... if you had been here, my brother would not have died.' Their implication is:

'Where were you? You weren't here when you were needed. Why didn't you come more quickly? You were too slow and now you are too late.'

What great lessons there are in this story for those whose prayers do not get answered! First, of course, Jesus wanted to demonstrate a resurrection – not a mere healing. Secondly, his goal was far greater than just to meet their needs with compassion. He wanted to strengthen their faith with a lesson they would never forget. God moves in a different realm of understanding, and he is never too late. But very often his ways are hidden from us, and this leads us to conclude that he has failed. Finally, of course, his motive is usually very different from ours, and part of the purpose of prayer is to give us the mind of Christ. Jesus' foremost desire was the reputation of his Father, not the health of Lazarus. 'Did I not tell you that if you believed, you would see the glory of God?' he said to the frustrated Martha, moments before her dead brother returned to life.

The purposes of prayer

Need I say that there is much more to prayer than expressing needs and receiving answers? Our perspective is so distorted by our fallen nature that the desire to 'get results from God' swells to gross proportions. In any case, God knows our needs before we ask. Our prayer relationship with God holds much more important significance. It is the heart of our contact with him. Prayer is where we come face to face with our own failure and fallenness, and find the wonder of God's generous acceptance. Prayer is where he can impart his mind and his character to us and mould us into the kind of people he wants us to be. Prayer is where God draws worship and love from our stony hearts.

We should not be surprised that prayer is a mysterious thing.

16

A World in Pain
The dilemma of suffering

The problem of suffering is as old as Genesis chapter 3, and there are no easy answers. What I find so problematic about suffering is not the experience of pain itself – if we humans are going to have feelings, it is inevitable we should have bad as well as good feelings. No. What really jars is why one person should suffer so much, for no obvious reason, and another escape unscathed. It is all so arbitrary and appears to be desperately unfair.

Harold Kushner, a Jewish rabbi, wrote a best-selling book entitled *When bad things happen to good people.*[206] He wanted to help people who had passed through the same sort of experience as he had faced with his son Aaron. In Aaron's first year of life it became evident that something was wrong with him, and at the age of three he was diagnosed as having a disease known as progeria, or 'rapid ageing'. It meant that he would never grow up to be a normal person. He would age abnormally quickly and begin to look like an old man while he was still a child. He would probably die in his early teens. Rabbi Kushner was devastated and tormented with questions.

> I had been a good person. I had tried to do what was right in the sight of God ... I believed I was following God's ways and doing His work. How could this be happening to my family? If God existed, if He was minimally fair, let alone loving and forgiving, how could He do this to me?[207]

The book was a best-seller because it struck a chord with many people who have struggled with the same questions.

In the mid-1960s when I was just launching out into evangelism, for several summers running I used to go door to door in northern France, selling Christian books and trying to share the gospel. Door after door was slammed in our faces, and the most common French words that were repeated in our ears every day were: '*Ça ne m'intéresse pas!*' – 'I am not interested!' When we had the opportunity to find out why so many people had no interest in Christ, the most common reason given was the War.

Here was a generation of French people who had grown up witnessing the most awful suffering and destruction, and it did not tally with their understanding of God. The Catholic Church stood apart as utterly irrelevant amidst the day-to-day horror of the people's pain. I sat on a bench in an open square in a French town once and struck up conversation with an old inhabitant. In the course of our conversation I asked him whether he believed in Jesus Christ.

The old man looked at me with hardened eyes, and then he turned and pointed to a large and rusty iron crucifix that stood at the edge of the square. He pointed to the crude figure of Jesus on the cross.

'Do you mean that gentleman there?' he said. 'I don't believe in him.'

Our problems come from the belief that God is good and that he is all-powerful, and the Bible appears to teach both those truths. If God were not good, but had some malicious and evil streak in his character that enjoyed watching the innocent suffer, then we would have no problem. Similarly, if he were not all-powerful and could therefore not prevent bad things from happening, we could understand and accept the state of affairs.

Rabbi Harold Kushner faced this dilemma and concluded that, though God is absolutely good and loving, he cannot be all-powerful:

If we have grown up ... believing in an all-wise, all-powerful, all-knowing God, it will be hard for us ... to change our way of thinking about Him ... But if we can bring ourselves to acknowledge that there are some things God does not control, many good things become possible.[208]

It is an easy and a satisfactory solution to an impossible dilemma, but I do not believe that it is an acceptable solution for those who accept the truth of God's Word. The Bible makes it amply clear that God is good and that he loves and cares for his creation. At the same time, God is absolutely sovereign and powerful and able to do all that he wills to do. He can divide the Red Sea overnight to allow his people to escape their sufferings. He can bring the dead back to life and restore the sick to health. He even has absolute authority over the activities of his great adversary Satan.

The only limitations on God's power are the self-limitations of his holiness and purity. He can do no evil. In his great wisdom, though he can certainly contradict the laws of nature, he normally chooses not to do so. It is a self-imposed limitation.

Psalm 73 and Job's comforters

The psalmist faced a similar dilemma when he wrote Psalm 73. He had been brought up to believe and accept certain theological niceties and he states them at the beginning of his poem:

Surely God is good to Israel, to those who are pure in heart.

It is what most Jews naturally believe and the Bible appears to teach. Job and his friends were brought up in the same theological school:

If you are pure and upright,
     even now he [God] will rouse himself on your behalf
and restore you to your rightful place.[209]

It is the theology of common sense, and the basis of all justice.

God rewards the good – and punishes those who are bad. But the agonized cry of both the psalmist and Job is that it doesn't work that way!

> the arrogant ... [and] the wicked ... have no struggles;
>   their bodies are healthy and strong.
> They are free from the burdens common to man;
>   they are not plagued by human ills.

God is manifestly unfair, the world is unfair and the psalmist is depressed, jealous and confused. I find it hard to believe that this is really a psalm of King Solomon – prosperous, satisfied and living most of his life in peace. This is the cry of someone who has done his best and found that life treated him badly, while he looked up and watched the wicked prospering. The fact is that the world is a terribly unfair and cruel place. Goodness is not rewarded and wickedness very often is.

Job's dilemma was similar but from a different angle. His condition demonstrated, according to his theology, that he must have committed some awful crime and was receiving the just desert for his behaviour. That is what his 'comforters' assumed. Their theology told them that it must be so. But the theology did not add up in his experience. Job knew that he had not committed crimes to deserve such suffering. His neat theological assumptions no longer made sense. God, the righteous One, was being desperately unfair.

A modern dilemma

I understand what the psalmist and Job are saying, and both of them gain spiritual credentials for absolute authenticity and sincerity. However, in our modern Western world I believe we face a different problem and it produces the same complex dilemma. It is a twenty-first-century version of the psalmist's cry.

Our problem is this. We Christians who live in the Western world have it so good. We spend millions on new church extensions, electronic equipment and comfortable seating. Our shelves are stacked with Bible commentaries, devotional books and spiritual materials of all kinds – teaching videos and worship CDs. We spend a fortune on attending conferences and Bible weeks, Christian holiday camps and luxury cruises.

If we fall ill, or face a crisis in our personal life, we know that we have access to reliable medical care, good doctors and hospitals, and in the case of a breakdown, psychological counsel and help are available. If things go wrong, we are covered by insurance. For most of us in this society it is not a matter of righteousness or evil. We have more than we need and it is usually available either from our own or from public resources.

We don't need to complain because the unrighteous win the lottery, because most of us also have enough and more than enough. Nor are we tempted to ask: *Why?* Why are we so prosperous and enjoy such plenty while our brothers and sisters in so much of the world really are suffering?

Watch the television screens night after night. As I write this, the dominant headline is Afghanistan, which has been deprived of sane government for two decades of civil war and still holds little promise of a decent life for its impoverished citizens. That competes in TV time with the tragedy of the Palestinian refugees and the mayhem caused by suicide bombers and Israeli retaliation. The sorrows of Kosovo were yesterday's headlines and before that Sierra Leone, where innocent people had their limbs hacked off by evil, drug-crazed 'rebels'. Our short memories still remember the utterly ruthless and cruel civil war between Chechen 'freedom fighters' and the Russian army in Chechnya – the pictures on our screens night after night of the tear-stained faces of ordinary women, whose sons had been killed and homes destroyed in the conflict. And the devastating floods in Mozambique, the violence in Sri Lanka, Eritrea and Ethiopia. Many of those who have suffered are Christians. Rwanda, which is still recovering from the genocide of a few years ago, is 80% Christian at least in name. The list is endless and today's tragedies will be supplanted by new disasters by the time you read these lines.

The tragedy and sorrow of these places does not go away when the journalists leave. The death and destruction just become overshadowed in the media by a new and greater crisis. Meanwhile we live our lives in peace and security, and do we ever ask *Why?* Why should we have it so easy, so comfortable? Why should we be so prosperous, able to worship the Lord and enjoy his blessings without the fear of hunger and drought, civil war and ethnic conflict? Did God create a First World to live in peace and stability, while the Third World lurches from crisis to crisis? Life is tragically unjust, painful and sad.

Job and the psalmist were Third World people, living at the bottom of the pile and looking up. True, Job was prosperous and had lived at ease, but he had no insurance policy, no free medical care, no clean and efficient hospital to take care of his sores. The dilemma they both faced was a brutal confrontation with the ruthless unfairness of life. 'Life' and God had treated them both cruelly, and they thought they deserved better.

It certainly is possible for us to have a Job experience and to feel that God is desperately unfair to us, but it is much harder for our brothers and sisters in the Third World. Why should we have it so good?

Life in a refugee camp

I have already written of my encounter with Mother Teresa in a Calcutta refugee camp. But there is another story from that time that is less attractive.

Every emergency attracts the curious, like flies to a dung heap, eager to see what is going on and feel part of the action. The East Pakistan crisis was no different and that was how I met Jim. That is not his real name, which I have happily forgotten. When I first visited him in his air-conditioned hotel room I found him sprawled across his bed in shorts, grossly overweight and smug. He and his demure companion had just flown in to look at the camps, and I had been deputed to take them around. I hoped that maybe they had a lot of money to give away, but they mainly wanted to take photographs.

The next day I took them to visit a camp outside the city. It was a humiliating experience. We parked our vehicle at a respectable distance and waded in among the refugees. We wandered around the muddy camp area looking at the pathetic rabble of uprooted humanity standing in the dirt around their scruffy shelters. Jim took some pictures, but it was on our way out of the camp that he spotted what he was really looking for. To maintain some sense of self-respect I tried to keep my distance from them, but Jim called me to come back. He needed help.

Jim had spotted the perfect refugee. He was standing alone some distance outside the main camp. He was naked apart from a loincloth and he was clearly close to his end. He was just a skeleton clothed in skin, his ribs outlined in detail, like the pictures from concentration camps. There was a dazed expression on his sad face.

Jim thrust his camera into my hands. Etched on my memory is an image of him adjusting his collar and pulling out a comb to run through his hair before he posed to have his picture taken beside the tragic Bengali refugee. I did my duty and have often wondered what use he made of that photo.

Later the same evening Jim and his friend took me to the Blue Fox nightclub in Park Street. I played my part and had a good meal. Jim was in his element, especially when he managed to persuade the attractive cabaret crooner to sing 'When the Saints go Marching In' for him. He looked on this success as some kind of spiritual achievement. After it was over I bade them goodbye and the next day they flew back to America. I have never heard from him since.

The scene is not only an ugly memory. It is a study in contrasts — the clash of First World Christianity with Third World misery. The clash of those who can afford to speak of the 'quality of life' with those who suffer on the brink of survival. How does a good God of love view such a scene? What justice is there in such inequality? What reason is there for such pain? Is it really God that is so unfair, so biased towards us?

Some say that God has 'blessed' the Western world because of its allegiance to Christianity, whereas the suffering and poverty of the Third World is a mark of his curse. Such arrogance and self-righteousness does not even merit comment.

There is no way we can equate that skinny refugee with righteous Job or the struggling psalmist, but the problems of pain in an unjust world are similar. Can God be good and allow such suffering to multiply unchecked?

Making sense of an unreasonable world

The psalmist went through moods like most of us do, but he also had the good sense to check himself and drag himself back from the brink of depression. After meditating rather fruitlessly on the agony of a world where evil is rewarded and the righteous suffer, he pulls himself together in verse 15:

> If I had said, 'I will speak thus,'
>   I would have betrayed your children.

'Hang on a moment,' he says to himself. 'I am talking nonsense. This kind of talk isn't going to do anybody any good. I accuse God of being unfair. Now I am myself being unfair to people who want help from me.'

It is a good moment for the psalmist. It is the turning point – from a period of destructive negative thinking to a more positive and constructive frame of mind. I know the feeling, because I am also by nature a negative thinker. If there is some bad thought to be had, I will surely have it.

'Solutions,' thought the psalmist, 'are more important than problems.' And here are the solutions the Lord gave him.

It's all a matter of perspective

> When I tried to understand all this,
>   it was oppressive to me

till I entered the sanctuary of God;
   then I understood their final destiny.

Perspective is everything, and our perspective is so limited that we are foolish to make a judgment until we can see the full picture. The Bible makes it plain that we cannot – and must not – judge the present except in the light of the future. We can only understand the era of time in the light of eternity. Even Jesus only endured the cross 'for the joy set before him'.[210]

There is indeed coming a Day of Reckoning, when all the injustices that trouble us so much here will be put right. On that day, and on that day alone, all the questions will be answered.

Many of us have lost that perspective, but it is an integral component of the Christian faith. We have perhaps been too influenced by the secular philosophies that have dominated the past century, and the materialism that pervades the present. Karl Marx's famous critique of Christianity carries a grain of truth: 'Religion is the sigh of the oppressed creature, the heart of a heartless world ... the opium of the people.' But his solution undermined all true hope: 'To abolish religion as the illusory happiness of the people is to demand their real happiness.'[211]

Marx threw the baby out with the bath-water. The promise of future hope should never become a substitute for working for present justice and happiness, but the Day of Judgment, when every wrong will be righted, is a fundamental Christian expectation. In its light today's suffering and injustice take on a very different appearance. What a different view we will have of present suffering when we look back at it from eternity! Jesus said:

Blessed are you who hunger now,
   For you will be satisfied ...
Woe to you who are well fed now,
   For you will go hungry ...[212]

One day this upside-down world is going to be turned right side up.

What a mess we have made of everything!

The psalmist had to confess what a fool he had been when he criticized God for the state of the world:

> When my heart was grieved,
>   and my spirit embittered,
> I was senseless and ignorant,
>   I was a brute beast before you.

All the problems began in the Garden of Eden, and again we must reaffirm that we cannot make sense of the present except in the light of this essential part of our history. Just as the present can only be understood in the perspective of the future, so also the present only makes sense when interpreted by the past.

Rabbi Harold Kushner has a chapter on Genesis 3 and the fall in his book,[213] but he misses the whole crucial point. Kushner believes that when Adam and Eve disobeyed God in the Garden, they entered a world of good and evil, in which people are free to make choices:

> Human beings live in a world of good and bad, and that makes our lives painful and complicated. Animals don't; their lives are much simpler, without the moral problems and moral decisions that we humans have to face.[214]

There is some truth in what he says, but the full truth is much more painful. That act of rebellion in the Garden had far wider consequences. The image of God was marred almost beyond recognition by the fall, the human mind became twisted, eyes were blinded and wills corrupted. Not only that, but Scripture teaches that nature itself was damaged, 'subjected to frustration'.[215] The very ground itself was cursed.[216] To ignore that is to miss the key that explains our situation.

We live in a cursed world that is still full of risks and dangers. It is useless to pretend that things are right when they are obviously wrong. But help is at hand and the promise of a new world is around the corner. A drowning person who cannot swim is a fool when he complains that the water is dangerous. Wisdom consists in crying for help.

My wife is convinced that she almost drowned when we were on holiday in France some years ago. No danger signs warned her that there were strong currents to beware of, but when she was some way from the shore – and still in fairly shallow water – she was caught in the strong tug of the current pulling her away from the beach and down under the water. She struggled in vain to swim but was soon out of her depth. At that moment she panicked, convinced that she was drowning, and cried in her heart, 'Jesus, help me!' Within moments she found our daughter beside her with a surfboard and shortly afterwards they were back in the shallows and could wade ashore.

It is a common experience and it doesn't always end so happily, but I hope it makes the point. God in his mercy has rescued us from our fate, and in his grace has promised us his glory. Who can argue with that?

The love of a Father

There is an inevitable next question to trouble us. In the light of the mess the world is in, and assuming that God has all power to rescue us from it, why in the name of all decency has he not done so?

The psalmist doesn't tackle that question and he doesn't provide an answer, but his next verse helps us to reach out towards a better understanding:

> Yet I am always with you;
> You hold me by my right hand.

Perhaps God could never adequately explain why he does not step in and sort out the mess, but what he has chosen to do is to affirm that he is not indifferent, and he does it by saying, 'It's okay. I am here with you. Hang on to me.' That can be more help for a troubled soul than any explanation. This was the psalmist's comfort in his moment of greatest agony, an insight into the true heart of a God who not only made us, but also wants us to be close to him. I too am a parent, and I know that there is no relationship quite as intimate, quite as strong, as that between parent and child.

An extraordinary thing is – and maybe this is all part of the consequences of the disaster in the Garden – the relationship between parent and child is probably one of the most difficult and stressful. Someone once said that 'The secret of bringing up children is not to be their parents.' Why is that?

I had a difficult relationship with my mother. She was the hardest person in the world for me to relax with and talk naturally to, though things improved as I grew older. I often tried to analyse it but never came up with a satisfactory answer. She was a strong character. She tried hard to impose her will on me, and I fought hard to resist her. That made it a difficult relationship. But there was more to it than that. The inborn desire and need to be free of our parents is a strong instinct in many children. Now I am a parent, I find the same difficulty exists with my offspring in relating to me.

Our relationship with our Father in heaven has similar tensions, but as a parent I can understand a little better the heart of God – love that will go to any extent, patience that will never be exhausted, and willingness to let go when we choose to be independent.

Why did God not wipe out his creation when it rebelled? I can understand why. Why does he not force us to submit and obey? I can understand that too. He is a wise parent, even if it has caused him endless pain. Harold Kushner has a chapter entitled 'God leaves us room to be human',[217] and that implies allowing us to hurt ourselves. But, when we do hurt ourselves, God, like any parent, is there to welcome and to comfort those in pain.

The personal touch

There is one further important factor that neither the psalmist nor Job – nor indeed Harold Kushner – had access to, which makes a world of difference. Twenty centuries ago God arrived on earth in Person, the ultimate expression of his desire to relate to us. And not only was Jesus fully human and able to sympathize with our weaknesses, but he was 'tempted in every way, just as we are – yet was without sin'.[218]

If only Job had lived a few hundred years later! So many of his dilemmas would have been resolved. The correct theology of his comforters failed to match his experience. He knew that God would understand his dilemma – if only he could confront him face to face!

Job was trapped between his personal tragedy, which made no sense to him, and the sense that God was indifferent. He wanted desperately to be able to argue his case with God. It all seemed so unfair:

> How can a mortal be righteous before God?
> Though one wished to dispute with him,
> He could not answer him one time out of a thousand.[219]

There is only one solution for Job – to be able to stand face to face with God, and have a referee who understands them both, one who can sympathize with Job's suffering and can also understand God's case against him.

> He is not a man like me that I might answer him,
> That we might confront each other in court.
> If only there were someone to arbitrate between us,
> To lay his hand upon us both.[220]

If only Job had known! And yet, in astonishing insight, he was convinced that God did understand him, and that one day God would vindicate his cause:

> I know that my Defender lives,
> and that in the end he will stand upon the earth,
> And after my skin has been destroyed,
> Yet in my flesh I will see God,
> I myself will see him with my own eyes – I and not
> another.[221]

Ancient Job had more insight into the plan of God for suffering people than many modern Christians! That Defender came many centuries later, lived as a mortal and ultimately died the death of a criminal, in order to save us – and also to say: 'God cares! God sympathizes! God has been through it all too!'

It is an amazing response to a very complex problem. Human suffering remains a mystery, probably one of the greatest mysteries we face, and we will never reconcile all the tensions and contradictions. But like so many of the questions and doubts that plague the thinking Christian, though we cannot see clearly through the cloud, at least the mist is parting, and it will all make sense on the other side.

17

Is That All?
The end of the beginning

Frank Peretti's novel *This Present Darkness* is one of the most exciting and readable Christian novels of recent years. We have already alluded to it in another context. It pictures life on two levels – the real world of Christians and criminals, and the supernatural world of angels and demons. Action aplenty takes place on both levels.

Susan Jacobson is not a Christian, but she is becoming increasingly aware of the spirit world and, as she gets more and more involved in the crooked dealings of the criminal underworld, so she increases in faith and begins to pray. She miraculously breaks out of captivity and escapes in a truck conveniently standing outside. A mighty battle ensues between the powers of good and evil over the progress of the little vehicle as it climbs the narrow, twisting mountain roads. In spite of the best efforts of the angels the conflict results in victory for the demons as the van finally crashes over a precipice and pitches down the mountainside, coming to rest in a pile of scrap and glass at the base of the mountain.

Something very similar happens to Kevin Weed, an old acquaintance of Susan who also becomes embroiled in the drama. Meeting up with two crooks in a tavern, his drink is laced with drugs in order to destroy him. As he drives away he is followed. His driving becomes increasingly erratic and finally his truck goes out of control and crashes into a deep river.

It is not the end of either Susan or Kevin. They still have an important role to play in the plot. But the reader is kept in suspense for forty-nine pages, assuming them both to be dead. Far from it! Susan re-emerges first, with the story that she had never got into the van nor had she driven over the mountain. Shortly afterwards Kevin also reappears.

'I thought for sure you were dead . . . your truck went into the river!'

'Yeah, I know. Some jerk stole it and crashed it. Somebody was trying to kill me . . . I was really spacing out, so I pulled over at Tucker's Burgers to throw up or get a drink of water or go to the bathroom or something. I fell asleep in the men's room, man, and I must have slept there all night. I woke up this morning and went outside and my truck was gone.'

So who had been in their vehicles when they crashed down the mountainside and nose-dived out of control into the river?

Kevin piped up, 'Hey, like maybe it was an angel that stole my truck.'[222]

It is marvellous story-telling – the world of angels and demons manipulating events and controlling the destiny of people unawares. Small wonder the book was on the best-seller lists. It is close enough to the truth to make us feel good about reading it, and close enough to real life to make us feel good about ourselves. And everything works out well in the end.

The only problem is that this is fiction. Because I believe the Bible, I believe in angels. I believe that they can and doubtless still do sometimes intervene in human affairs. But normally they don't.

Back to reality

I had recently arrived back in Britain after a very eventful few years in India. Our work in India had been going very well and had recently focused on a massive evangelistic programme in the northern State of Uttar Pradesh, known as Reach UP. At one point I had been asked to co-ordinate this programme, but due to events beyond my control it became impossible. A close friend from New Zealand, Chris Begg, took over the huge task of overseeing the programme.

Chris and I were close friends. We had travelled to India together seven years earlier and worked in eastern India. He was a gifted musician and song-writer, and very popular in the Calcutta churches. Chris and I both married Swedish girls on the same day in 1972 – he in India and I in Sweden.

After the Reach UP programme in India, Chris and his wife Hillevi had planned a well-earned break in Europe and they set out with four others in a Volkswagen minibus to drive back overland. It was a journey that was quite familiar to us in those days, as the cheapest and most convenient way between Europe and India.

I received the news at home in early December, when the telephone rang and Chris's mother spoke to me. 'Chris and Hillevi have been killed,' she said. It took some time to understand what she was saying and it took months to sink in. They had been young, talented, enthusiastic, full of life and promise. Driving through Yugoslavia, they had just stopped for a meal and were driving on in the dark. It was late evening, and they hit a mammoth transcontinental truck head on. Four people were killed in the vehicle, but it was the death of Chris and Hillevi that made the deepest impact on me.

This was real life. There was no angel to take control of the wheel at the moment of danger. Such things only happen in fiction. In reality, people die, whether they are innocent or guilty, young or old, married or single.

The son of a friend in Calcutta had died some months earlier, and as is the custom, I went to offer my condolences to his family. The body was laid out on a bed under a fan. He was dressed in a white *kurta* and *pyjama*, which fluttered in the breeze from the fan. We sat on chairs around the bed in silence, looking at the body and contemplating the mystery of death. I remember praying and in my imagination wondering what would happen if (as in the case of Jairus' daughter or the Shunammite's son in the book of Kings)[223] he had suddenly sneezed and sat up. He didn't.

Death is around us all the time and the older we grow, the more familiar we become with its visits. Medical science and skill 'saves' many lives, but death always wins in the end. It is the great inevitability.

My mother died in 1977 while I was away. I flew back for the funeral. Mother had been so strong, so indestructible, so permanent, and now she was gone. I came into my own home and she was no longer there. There were oranges in the fruit bowl, which she must have bought just a few days earlier, but she never had time to eat them, and never would. Death held an incomparable and deeply tragic finality, and that is its inescapable reality. There is no going back, no fast replay, no second chance.

The last great enemy

As a Christian I believe in the resurrection of the dead. I believe that Jesus Christ came out of the tomb where his dead body had been buried after the crucifixion and, incredible as it may seem, appeared alive and well to his followers.

And yet still my mind insists that such things do not happen. They are impossible. Death by definition means the end. I had a close friend who committed suicide a few months ago. In a moment of despair he threw himself in front of a railway train. In his mind he must have thought, 'I'm going to end it all.' That is what our instinct tells us – that after death ... nothing more.

As we have turned the corner into the twenty-first century, one of the questions that keeps being asked is whether science (that wonderful deity) will be able to prolong our lives, perhaps indefinitely. 'Can I live to 125?' asked a lead article in *Time* magazine at the end of the old century.[224] 'Some scientists predict that by 2100, our descendants could live to be 200 years of age.'

The BBC *Horizon* programme showed a film on the same theme entitled *Living Forever*.

It's humanity's oldest dream – immortality. A world where we never age. A world where death will be purely optional. And a handful of scientists believe that this really will be our future.

Central to the programme was the aspiration of a sad old man, a Texan oil millionaire who claimed to enjoy life so much that he had offered a fortune to anyone who could prevent him from dying. I felt sorry for this pathetic elderly millionaire coming to the end of his life totally unprepared. Scientists are working overtime to devise ways of reversing the ageing processes, or replacing organs and tissues as they wear out in order to defy the laws of nature. 'I really do believe that it is theoretically possible to have absolute immortality – barring accidents,' said one researcher. It looks like a replay of Mary Shelley's *Frankenstein*, but some are pinning great hopes on it.

An eighty-five-year-old woman wrote an article under the heading 'Alone and Awake' in *The Oldie* magazine. It was heavy with sadness, expressing the hopelessness that goes with the common philosophy of our day:

Insomnia for me is a loneliness in the night, when life seems to have let go of my hand, leaving me in a maze of melancholic thoughts which I cannot control or switch off.

At the age of thirty-four her father was killed in a mining accident. That 'killed for ever in me the belief that some omnipotent, just God was keeping an eye on the human race'. One personal tragedy followed another, culminating in the death of her husband of sixty years, 'silently, without a struggle, in his sleep – with no chance to say goodbye ...'

Over the years I had cleansed his tortured mind of the idea that he would go to the Catholic Hell ... I was humble enough to accept the fact I was not worth any reincarnation ... but egotistical enough to feel furious that we were given enough brains to be curious about existence but not enough brains to know why we were part of it.[225]

One old man pins his hopes on a scientific breakthrough to enable him to live for ever. Another lives in the dread of being extinguished like a candle in the night without purpose or meaning. It all looks pretty depressing and it underscores a great and important fact – that death is the last great enemy, which everyone looks to with dread. Why? Because it is so unclear what lies beyond it, and most assume that there is nothing there that is more attractive than what we have here. After all, a bird in the hand is worth any number in the bush.

I have caught myself saying to someone, whose father had just died, 'I am so sorry to hear that your dad has gone to be with the Lord.' That is practical unbelief. I should be glad that someone has gone to be with Christ, instead of facing a bleak and terrifying eternity alone or something even worse. The one who dies with faith in Christ can only gain, according to what we say we believe.

In practical terms most of us put all our eggs (or as many eggs as possible) in the one basket we know about for sure – the basket of life. This is in stark contrast to the teaching of Jesus: 'Do not store up for yourselves treasures on earth ... but store up for yourselves treasures in heaven ...'[226]

Those who follow the teaching of the prosperity movement could be accused of being among the greatest unbelievers of all. Their teaching emphasizes that God wants to give us everything – health and wealth, success and protection – all here and now. No need to wait for the future.

I have to be careful here, because God has given us a lot of promises for the present here and now – joy, peace, 'every spiritual blessing in the heavenly places'[227] and much more besides. It is important to note that most of those promises to the New Testament saints are spiritual blessings and not material. They relate to our inner condition, and not our outer well-being. But that is not exclusively so. Jesus made a promise to those who have made sacrifices to follow him. They will receive 'a hundred times as much in this present age [homes, brothers, sisters, mothers, children and fields – and then he adds the sting in the tail – "and with them persecutions"] and in the age to come, eternal life'.[228]

Constantly the Scriptures take us back to the great purpose of life – 'the age to come'. Our present life only makes sense in the age to come. And that lies beyond the grave.

Do I believe in that? Or does it still scare me out of my wits? My natural self is still eager to hold onto all that I can see, taste and touch. I don't want to leave it all behind. It is substantial and real. I am scared that when I die I will lose it all. Another part of me says, 'Thank God for the glory that lies beyond the grave.'

When I was in Pakistan some years ago I developed a lump on my wrist. I didn't know what it was but it made me nervous. One hears so much about lumps that turn out to be malignant. For a moment I thought, 'This is it. This could be the great test of my life.' Would I be a practical atheist or be able to look forward to what lay ahead?

I took it to the doctor and he dismissed it with a medical name and said to me, 'The old medical books tell you to hit it with the family Bible and it will disappear.' He charged me thirty rupees for the advice. I went home, hit it with a Bible and the lump disappeared.

But I had become a fraction wiser in the process.

The hope of resurrection

In an article in *The Sunday Telegraph* just after Easter 2000 Auberon Waugh wrote the following:

Of all the great feasts of the church, Easter places the worst strain on the faith of modern Christians. Traditional answers to the question of why the Crucifixion was necessary in the first place do not help to resolve the second great doubt, about whether the Resurrection was an historical event, whether a dead body actually returned to life. Christians, who begin to ask themselves if the Crucifixion was really necessary, if the Resurrection really occurred, are only a step away from asking themselves if Jesus Christ was really God, a member of the mysterious Trinity, or just a charismatic Jewish preacher of the first century.[229]

It is a wise and perceptive statement. Waugh discerns that our faith hangs on the historical truth of the crucifixion and the resurrection. If they are a myth, then Jesus' claims to deity fall flat. He is no more than a charismatic Jewish preacher who managed to mesmerize his disciples.

He is right too to say that it takes considerable strain to believe in the bodily resurrection of Christ. Modern people, trained in the mind-set of scientific rationalism, do not accept virgin births, miraculous healings and stories of people walking on water. Such things not only do not happen – they cannot happen. Still less can someone who has been beaten, nailed to a piece of wood to hang in the sun till he is certified dead, before having a spear stuck in his side, come back to life again after three days. It is not scientifically acceptable.

And yet all the available evidence points to the fact that, in the case of Jesus of Nazareth, it did happen! We examined a fraction of the evidence in Chapter 7, and many books have been written by capable and qualified people that provide a stronger case.

I believe that, apart from the written evidence, probably the greatest proof is to be found in the healthy survival of the Christian church 2,000 years later. All it would have taken to finish off the new sect of Christ-followers would have been for someone to produce his dead body. They didn't, because it was nowhere to be found. The little group of discouraged disciples had been radically transformed into a fervent band of enthusiastic followers who were willing to go to any lengths to tell the world that Jesus was alive.

As Auberon Waugh so clearly indicates, believe in the truth of the resurrection, and it is but a small step to believe in the deity of Christ and the whole marvellous package of the gospel. Deny the resurrection (as some people do who should know better), and the whole pack of cards looks very ready to collapse.

Furthermore, if Jesus Christ really rose from the tomb, as so much available evidence indicates, then that opens up a whole extraordinary new chapter for us as well. For Jesus said, 'Because I live, you also will live.'[230]

> I am the resurrection and the life. He who believes in me will live, even though he dies; and whoever lives and believes in me will never die. Do you believe this?[231]

Between heaven and earth

One of the most extraordinary things about the writers of the Bible is the way they appear able to accept so nonchalantly the existence of the divine, invisible world. God, the angels, eternity and future glory are taken for granted. In the most natural way, writer after writer is able to slip between the visible and the invisible worlds with astonishing ease. What today seems to be so unusual, these people took for granted.

The book of Revelation is the most obvious example. In chapter 1 John is 'on the island of Patmos'[232] in the Mediterranean. In an instant – the next verse – 'on the Lord's Day I was in the Spirit' and he sees a vision of the Lord Jesus Christ in all his present splendour, quite unlike anything he has ever seen before.

In chapter 4 he is in heaven – 'I looked, and there before me was a door standing open in heaven' – and for two whole chapters he marvels at the vision of the throne of God and its environment.

In chapter 6 he is back on the earth where he has a vision of the beginnings of judgment. The next chapter also begins on the earth, where he sees the servants of God who have been sealed (protected) with the mark of the living God, and then without warning at verse 9, 'I looked and there before me was a great multitude ... standing before the throne.' So it continues, a great drama with scenes alternating between heaven and earth.

The amazing thing about all this is that those who are in heaven – 'those who had been slain because of the word of God and the testimony they had maintained' [233] – are just as much alive as those who are on the earth and have not yet died!

The doorway we call 'Death' is, for the believer, just that – a doorway into another, fuller, richer life.

> Where, O death, is your victory?
> Where, O death, is your sting? [234]

D. L. Moody was an outstanding preacher and evangelist of the nineteenth century. At the end of a long life of exhausting service for God, as he contemplated the end of his life on earth, he wrote:

> Some day you will read in the papers that Moody is dead. Don't you believe a word of it. At that moment I shall be more alive than I am now. [235]

When he came to die, with his family gathered about his bed, he was perfectly content and ready to go. 'No, this is no dream ... It is beautiful ... If this is death it is sweet. God is calling me and I must go,' he said. 'Don't hold me back ... This is my coronation day. I have been looking forward to it for years.'

That, surely, is the Christian hope and affirmation of life. While we have life, we can live it to the full, and ahead lies the Great Adventure. Not to fear death is the Christian's privilege. It confirms the truth of our unique faith.

18

Drawing in the Net
Still wondering

Some years ago a sensational news report claimed that the tomb of Jesus had been discovered in Jerusalem. Archaeologists digging in the earth came across memorial slabs bearing the name 'JESUS'. Maybe they even found some bones. They made the most of the discovery to claim their moment of fame, and then the report sank into oblivion.

But what if it had been true? Obviously, if such a discovery were to be made, it would most likely have been done long ago by the authorities, who needed so badly to quash the rumours that Jesus was alive. The Christian faith has always had people who wished to disprove it. There has never been a period in history when people have not tried to deny, destroy or distort the claims of Jesus. But what if one day someone succeeded, and beyond all possibility of doubt demonstrated that he was a fraud and the Christian faith a lie?

It is the stuff of nightmares. But what if it happened?

Were it ever proven that Jesus Christ was a fraud, honest Christians would need to apologize and leave the church. It would be foolish to continue to love an ideal, knowing it to be non-existent. And yet, if it were ever finally proven that there is no God and that Christ was a fraud – albeit the greatest and most brilliant fraud the world has ever seen – the world would be tempted to invent him to fill the void that would be created.

Two millennia of our history and culture would need to be reassessed, such has been the impact of Jesus' teaching and Christian influence on our world. Our present era tries to act on the assumption that God is a myth and religion largely irrelevant, but in reality the foundations of our society are still built upon Judeo-Christian thought. It would be profoundly disturbing to discover that those foundations were based on a lie.

The loss of meaning

Suddenly we would become very lonely animals, spinning through space on a very insignificant bit of mud, heading nowhere. Strangely enough, we are intelligent enough to be able to be terrified by the thought of meaninglessness and insignificance.

Happiness, whatever that meant, would therefore be just a matter of chemical reactions that provide momentary good feeling. Nevertheless, those good feelings would become the highest 'good', and the best thing we could hope for in life would be to have a lot of them.

Is it any wonder that people long for significance – even while smart secularists work overtime to undermine all hope of meaning? Is it any surprise that suicide is rising fastest in the most developed, and most secular, countries of the world? In 1998, 32,863 Japanese people committed suicide – three times the number of deaths through road accidents.[236] Why?

Professor Richard Dawkins runs a personal crusade to disillusion people about God. In the BBC TV series *The Soul of Britain*[237] he stated:

Of course I am unhappy to be living in a society where I think a majority of people are deluded and I would love to do something about that ... I think science really has fulfilled a need that religion did in the past of explaining things, explaining why we are here, what is the origin of life, where did the world come from, what is life all about ...

Professor Dawkins tragically overestimates the achievements of science in his zeal to enlighten his fellow man. Science indeed wonderfully explains *how* things happen and *how* we got here. But it is not the business of science to begin to explain *why* they happen, nor *why* we are here.

But what if Professor Dawkins' vision of a godless, empty universe were right? What if every phenomenon could be explained scientifically as cause and effect, without meaning, without direction? What if this were truly a closed universe?

In a world ruled by scientific determinism, would there be any room left for morality? for virtue? for principle? for beauty? Would we all have to admit that Lenin's answer was the most logical? or Stalin's? or Hitler's? In a world without God, their logic – and their cruelty – would be not at all unreasonable.

Other questions that demand an answer

I find myself asking questions not only when I read the Bible. There are other questions – big questions about the world and those around me – that bug me no less. The only difference is that very often the answers seem to be much more obvious.

Think, for example, of the conflict between India and Pakistan that has claimed the lives of thousands over more than half a century. Why are the politicians so stupid? Why can they not sit down together and discuss rationally a fair division of the land? What is the point of killing one another over a matter of principle and a few miles of soil? Why can they not agree to a compromise – throw open the borders and allow the peoples of these two nations to cross freely and live in friendship?

I can assure you it won't happen, barring a miracle. Why? Because there is vested interest in continued conflict, and a huge ocean of irrational bitterness, national and religious pride, that makes peace and progress impossible. The way these two opposing nations behave – and threaten each other with nuclear destruction – is evidence that the Bible's diagnosis of human selfishness and sin is absolutely accurate. The Bible makes a good point when it insists that the only answer is to repent and prostrate themselves in humility before God, if they want the problem to be solved.

Think again of the optimistic hopes that the ethnic Albanians and the Kosovar Serbs would quickly put their differences behind them, forgive each other for their past misdeeds, and decide to create a new state where peoples of all races and religions could live together in peace and harmony. Think of the dream of a new Afghanistan where brother Pathan can live in love and harmony with brother Tajik, free from the dominance of warlords and ethic conflict. Such dreams make a lot of sense, don't they? Why live in bitterness and hatred, when forgiveness and love make one so much happier?

It does not take long to realize that it is wise and courageous to hope, but vain to dream. No-one puts away the desire for revenge quickly, even if logic proclaims that it is the way to peace and happiness. The Balkans and Afghanistan have been mired in ethnic tension for centuries, a vivid illustration of the Bible's image of humanity in urgent need of outside help.

Dare I touch on the conflict in Northern Ireland? I am painfully aware that few outside the Province can understand the complexities of the situation. But every time I watch on my TV screen the stubbornness of the Loyalists and the equal obstinacy of the Catholic community, I think how easily the problem could be solved if both sides would humbly back down, practise some courtesy and count each other as better than themselves. Why can't the Orangemen decide to take their parades to a different street? Or the residents of the Garvaghy Road in Drumcree agree to stay at home and let the marchers have their parade? Or, better still (and to be sure to win the moral high ground), why don't they come out to cheer them on? Problem solved.

I know it is not so simple and it probably won't happen. Why? Because the hearts of people, both Catholic and Protestant, are still riddled with pride and a determination to stand up for their rights! And what are their rights before almighty God?

The glorious alternative

A report in the June 1999 newsletter of the Mennonite Church Peace and Justice Committee in South Africa gave an example of the glorious alternative – the Christian answer to the human dilemma. It told of the trial of a white police officer, a certain Mr van der Broek, who was accused of complicity in the murder of two black men some years before.

Facing the accused was a frail black lady, seventy years of age, whose husband and son had been murdered by the two accused officers. The court established that Mr van der Broek had come to the old lady's home, taken her son, shot him and burned his body while he and his officers joked together. Several years later, her husband had been taken away by the same Mr van der Broek. The old lady had then been taken to witness his brutal killing by white police officers. After being beaten and bound, he had been doused in gasoline and set on fire. The report continues:

> And now the woman stands in the courtroom and listens to the confessions offered by Mr van der Broek. A member of South Africa's Truth and Reconciliation Commission turns to her and asks, 'So, what do you want? How should justice be done to this man who has so brutally destroyed your family?'
>
> 'I want three things,' begins the old woman calmly, but confidently. 'I want first to be taken to the place where my husband's body was burned so that I can gather up the dust and give his remains a decent burial.'
>
> She pauses, then continues. 'My husband and son were my only family. I want, secondly, therefore, for Mr van der Broek to become my son. I would like for him to come twice a month to the ghetto and spend a day with me so that I can pour out on him whatever love I still have remaining within me.'
>
> 'And, finally,' she says, 'I want a third thing. I would like Mr van der Broek to know that I offer him my forgiveness because Jesus Christ died to forgive. This was also the wish of

my husband. And so, I would kindly ask someone to come to my side and lead me across the courtroom so that I can take Mr van der Broek in my arms, embrace him and let him know that he is truly forgiven.'

As the court assistants come to lead the elderly woman across the room, Mr van der Broek, overwhelmed by what he has just heard, faints. And as he does, those in the courtroom, friends, family, neighbours – all victims of decades of oppression and injustice – begin to sing, softly, but assuredly, 'Amazing grace, how sweet the sound, that saved a wretch like me.'[238]

What if Professor Dawkins' vision of a rational world that had abolished faith in God were to come to pass? What if the supernatural and the divine were disproved, and Jesus shown to be a fraud and a cheat who had deceived the world?

What if such courageous examples of the nobility of the human spirit were just trivial wasted breath?

Questions aside

The disciples once came to Jesus and said to him: 'Who is the greatest in the kingdom of heaven?'

Jesus replied: 'I tell you the truth, unless you change and become like little children, you will never enter the kingdom of heaven. Therefore, whoever humbles himself like this child is the greatest in the kingdom of heaven.'[239]

There comes a time when questions must be set aside. True greatness does not consist in having great intelligence, nor in having an answer to every question. It comes from humility and trust.

In my rooms on the third floor of number 26, Trinity College Dublin, on 30 October 1962, I came to the conclusion that all my questions would never be answered, and I had to take a step of faith. Not a step into the dark, but a personal commitment on the basis of what I knew and believed to be true.

And in setting aside my hesitations and my procrastinations for that moment, I discovered in a way that no logic could ever have revealed, that God was there, his Word could be trusted and Jesus Christ was indeed the Light of the world.

'Lord, I believe. Help my unbelief!'

Where Do We Go from Here?
Read on . . .

In no way is the following a complete list of the books that have helped me to cling to my faith. At best this is a survey of a few of the volumes that have encouraged me and might well encourage others, in dealing with some of those persistent mosquitoes. One thing is sure – the more we read, the better we understand.

1. Faith in Context
I begin with several books that cover a wide range of issues concerning our world and spiritual reality.

> Charles Colson & Nancy Pearson, *How Now Shall We Live?* (Marshall Pickering)

Every book I have read by Chuck Colson has strengthened my conviction that the Christian faith is true. *How Now Shall We Live?* is a masterful analysis of the modern world and the logic of biblical belief in the midst of cultural turmoil. C. S. Lewis had a momentous influence on Chuck Colson, and his books are still unequalled in their insight into the failings of humanity and our need for God.

> C. S. Lewis, *Mere Christianity* (Fount/HarperCollins)
> C. S. Lewis, *Surprised by Joy* (Fount/HarperCollins)

Books of general apologetics that set out the evidence and logic of Christianity are invaluable faith-builders and mosquito-killers. John Stott helped me to come to faith in 1962 and his *Basic Christianity* was the first Christian book I ever bought. It is still in print. Josh McDowell has written a library of apologetic books, all well researched and readable.

John R. W. Stott, *Basic Christianity* (Inter-Varsity Press)
Josh McDowell, *Evidence that Demands a Verdict* (Scripture Press and Alpha)

In a general pastoral category, I must recommend the books of Philip Yancey. He makes a profession of honest evaluation and his writings have given fresh insights into many old problems.

Philip Yancey, *Reaching for the Invisible God* (Zondervan)
Philip Yancey, *I was just wondering* (Eagle)

The latter volume is definitely written for church mosquito-killers. Yancey describes it as 'a book of many questions and a few answers'.

2. Cerebral Faith
John R. W. Stott, *Your Mind Matters* (Inter-Varsity Press)

Stott's booklet is short and concise, but contains lucid and sound arguments for the essential place of the mind in establishing and affirming faith.

3. Where on Earth is God?
David Wilkinson, *God, Time and Stephen Hawking* (Monarch Books)

Many books set out the arguments for the existence of a deity, some more convincing than others. I found Wilkinson particularly helpful as he is himself an established representative of the scientific community.

4. Finding Your Way
5. So Many Books
6. Making Sense of the Book
Early in my Christian life I began to ask the question: How can I

know that the Bible is reliable and that the Bible alone is the true Word of God? A small booklet by Michael Green started me on my quest for answers to this crucial question. That is now out of print, but many other books give equally sound answers that are both scholarly and readable.

Francis A. Schaeffer, *Trilogy* (Inter-Varsity Press)
J. I. Packer, *God Has Spoken* (Hodder & Stoughton)
John Wenham, *Christ and the Bible* (Eagle)
F. F. Bruce, *The New Testament Documents: Are they reliable?* (Inter-Varsity Press)

7. Why Jesus?

The person and nature of Jesus is one of the great cornerstones of the Christian faith, without which no faith is possible. Several books have strengthened my conviction that we are right to focus so much on him.

Josh McDowell, *More than a Carpenter* (Kingsway)
John Pollock, *Jesus the Master* (Kingsway)

As so much hinges on whether Jesus is dead or alive today, evidence for his resurrection is of special interest. There are many books on this issue that are worth reading, and most of them are faith-builders.

Norman Anderson, *Evidence for the Resurrection* (Inter-Varsity Press)
Michael Green, *The Empty Cross* (Hodder & Stoughton)

8. Only One Way

Pluralism is the acceptable philosophy of our day – but is it correct and true? In our post-modern age, what is truth? Good questions need specially good answers.

Josh McDowell & Bob Hostetler, *The New Tolerance* (Tyndale House)
Douglas R. Groethuis, *Truth Decay* (Inter-Varsity Press)

Josh McDowell gives an invaluable insight into some fundamental post-modern world-views. Douglas Groethuis is harder to read but presents a sounder refutation of much post-modern theory in healthy defence of the truth.

The subject of hell should trouble us all, but some books provide helpful insights and compassionate understanding of what the Bible really teaches.

J. David Pawson, *The Road to Hell* (Hodder & Stoughton)
Dick Dowsett, *God, That's not fair!* (OM Publishing)
Evangelical Alliance, *The Nature of Hell* (ACUTE)

9. Sums That Don't Add Up
Philip Yancey, *Soul Survivor* (Hodder & Stoughton)

Philip Yancey's insights into the church are both painful and stimulating. He introduces this book with the confession: 'I have spent most of my life in recovery from the church.'

10. Over the Top
11. The World of Make-Believe
Sadly, I have not found many helpful books on this awkward subject, but a few deal with heresies and distortions in the church which we need to know about. Sometimes the criticisms of dishonesty themselves suffer from exaggeration and distortion, but I found these books especially helpful:

Florence Bulle, *The Many Faces of Deception* (Bethany House)
Hank Hanegraaff, *Christianity in Crisis* (Harvest House Publishers)

12. An Unfair World
Questions of world poverty and the unfair distribution of the world's resources should trouble every conscientious person. Without labouring under guilt, Ronald Sider has helped many Christians to try to live more responsibly.

Ronald Sider, *Rich Christians in an Age of Hunger* (Hodder & Stoughton)
Dewi Hughes, *God of the Poor* (OM Publishing)

214 CAN IT BE TRUE?

13. Does God Care?

No sincere Christian can afford to neglect the task of missions and the worldwide growth of the church. Further reading on what is happening around the world can only help us to respond suitably. Patrick Johnstone, author of *Operation World*, is well placed to give a broad overview.

> Patrick Johnstone, *The Church is Bigger Than You Think* (Christian Focus Publications)
> J. Oswald Sanders, *What of the Unevangelized?* (Christian Focus Publications)

14. Signs and Wonders

Many books have been written about power – power to be holy, power for living, power for signs and wonders. Most are very idealistic and hold out great promise and hope for an experience of the supernatural. Few books give a truly realistic and balanced perspective on power in the Christian life.

> Richard Foster, *Money, Sex and Power* (Hodder & Stoughton)
> Geoffrey Lay, *Seeking Signs and Missing Wonders* (Monarch Books)

15. Unanswered Prayer

There will never be a fully satisfactory answer to why God does not answer some of our sincere prayers. Most books on prayer provide simplistic formulae and challenge us to great prayer commitment. Ronald Dunn, however, writes from painful experience.

> Ronald Dunn, *When Heaven is Silent* (Word)
> C. S. Lewis, *Prayer: Letters to Malcolm* (Fount/HarperCollins)
> Richard Foster, *Prayer* (Hodder & Stoughton)

16. A World in Pain

While few books deal with unanswered prayer adequately, many tackle the problem of suffering. Somehow, it seems, answers are easier to find. All the books below are helpful.

Alister McGrath, *Why Does God Allow Suffering?* (Hodder & Stoughton)
Philip Yancey, *Where is God When it Hurts?* (Zondervan)
Warren W. Wiersbe, *When Life Falls Apart* (Spire)

17. Is That All?
Death is not a popular subject, but it is a reality we all need to be ready for. The Christian faith has a significant focus on death – and an even more significant promise of resurrection and life beyond the grave.

Billy Graham, *Death and the Life After* (Word)
Harold Bauman, *Living Through Grief* (Lion)

Finally, I probably gain my greatest encouragement from the reading of Christian (and non-Christian) biographies. I realize that every biography is distorted somewhat and needs to be taken with a pinch of salt. But, with that proviso, I strongly recommend a small selection of the many that have blessed and encouraged me.

John Pollock, *Moody without Sankey* (Christian Focus Publications)
John Pollock, *Hudson Taylor and Maria* (Christian Focus Publications)
Charles Colson, *Born Again* (Hodder & Stoughton)
Richard Wurmbrand, *Tortured for Christ* (Hodder & Stoughton)

Notes

1. 2 Timothy 4:7.
2. 2 Corinthians 4:8.
3. Matthew 22:37.
4. Luke 24:45.
5. J. R. W. Stott, *Your Mind Matters* (Inter-Varsity Press, Leicester, 1972), p. 60.
6. 1 Peter 3:15.
7. Acts 17:11.
8. Numbers 36.
9. Ephesians 1:19.
10. Roy Clements, *Songs of Experience* (Christian Focus Publications, Fearn, 1993), p. 74.
11. 2 Corinthians 6:15.
12. Hebrews 3:1–2.
13. Luke 24:4 RSV.
14. 2 Corinthians 4:8.
15. Acts 2:12.
16. Clements, op. cit., p. 74.
17. Figures quoted in *The Sunday Telegraph*, 28 May 2000.
18. Broadcast speech of 18 June 1940, from Winston Churchill, *Great War Speeches* (Corgi Books, London, 1957), p. 37.
19. *The Daily Telegraph*, 8 November 1999.
20. *The Daily Telegraph*, 24 June 2001, citing *The Values Debate – A Voice from the Pupils* (Woburn Press).
21. Article in *The Plain Truth*, April–May 2000.
22. Ibid., quoting from *The Guardian*, 29 May 1999.

23. Raymond A. Moody, Jr, *Life after Life* (Bantam, New York, 1976).
24. Elizabeth Kubler-Ross, *On Death and Dying* (MacMillan, New York, 1969).
25. A brief but excellent critique of Moody and Kubler-Ross can be found in Florence Bulle, *The Many Faces of Deception* (Bethany House, Minneapolis, 1983), pp. 162–174.
26. Psalm 14:1–2.
27. Isaiah 8:19.
28. *Alien Empire*, produced by Steve Nicholls for BBC Bristol, 1996.
29. *Time*, 13 August 2001.
30. David Wilkinson, *God, Time and Stephen Hawking* (Monarch Books, London and Grand Rapids, 2001), p. 147.
31. Ibid., p. 148.
32. Psalm 19:1.
33. C. S. Lewis, *Surprised by Joy* (Fount, London, 1977), pp. 136–137.
34. Acts 2:17.
35. 1 Corinthians 14:1.
36. The Roman Catholic Bible contains the 17 so-called Apocryphal (meaning 'hidden') Books, which were rejected by the Reformers in the sixteenth century because their authorship was held in question.
37. Brooks Alexander, 'Virtuality and Theophobia', ch. 8 in *Virtual Gods*, ed. Tal Brooke (Harvest House Publishers, Eugene, Oregon, 1997), p. 169.
38. Hebrews 11:6.
39. 1 John 4:1.
40. See 1 John 3:14, for example.
41. 2 John 10.
42. Published by the Islamic Propagation Centre International (Birmingham).
43. Hebrews 1:1.
44. 2 Timothy 3:16.

45. J. I. Packer, *God has Spoken* (Hodder & Stoughton, London, 1965), p. 14.
46. John 10:35.
47. John 16:13.
48. Galatians 1:8.
49. Romans 1:20.
50. Romans 2:15.
51. Acts 17:23–29.
52. Daniel 4:2.
53. Isaiah 45:1.
54. 1 Corinthians 2:11–12.
55. Luke 24:45.
56. 1 Chronicles 9:1.
57. J. B. Phillips, *The Ring of Truth* (Hodder & Stoughton, London, 1967).
58. Matthew 7:16, 18.
59. Exodus 32:28.
60. 1 Samuel 15:33 RSV.
61. 1 Chronicles 21.
62. 1 Chronicles 13:9.
63. *The Sunday Telegraph*, 23 January 2000.
64. *The Soul of Britain*, BBC TV, June 2000.
65. *Art that Shook the World*, BBC TV, 5 May 2001.
66. Genesis 14:17–24.
67. Genesis 15:12.
68. Genesis 18.
69. Genesis 31:42.
70. 1 Timothy 6:16.
71. 1 John 1:5.
72. Exodus 20:21.
73. Exodus 33:19–20.
74. Ezekiel 1:28.
75. Isaiah 6:1–5.
76. Isaiah 5:26.
77. 1 Timothy 6:16.
78. Acts 17:28.
79. John 11:21–26.

80. Compare John 3:13 (these are loose paraphrases, but the meaning is clear).
81. Compare John 14:3–5.
82. Compare John 14:6.
83. John 10:7 RSV.
84. John 14:9.
85. John 1:18 RSV.
86. Colossians 1:15.
87. Colossians 1:19.
88. John 21:7.
89. Quoted in Josh McDowell, *Evidence that Demands a Verdict* (Scripture Press, Amersham-on-the-hill, UK, 1990), p. 105.
90. Quoted in McDowell, op. cit., p. 106.
91. *The First Gospel of the Infancy of Jesus Christ*, 1:2–3.
92. Ibid., 3:6–8.
93. Matthew 8:27.
94. John 5:12, 18.
95. John 6:41–42.
96. John 8:53, 58.
97. 1 Corinthians 15:14–20.
98. 1 Corinthians 15:6.
99. See the list of recommended books for a small selection.
100. C. S. Lewis, *Surprised by Joy* (Fount, London, 1998), p. 178.
101. Ibid., pp. 183–184.
102. 1 Corinthians 15:20.
103. John 14:6.
104. Josh McDowell and Bob Hostetler, *The New Tolerance* (Tyndale House Publishers, Wheaton, 1998), pp. 2, 19.
105. *The Sunday Telegraph*, 5 August 2001.
106. Acts 17:24–33.
107. 1 Timothy 2:5.
108. Matthew 7:13–14.
109. Dale Carnegie, author of *How to Win Friends and Influence People*.
110. Revelation 19:20; 20:10.

111. Matthew 8:12.
112. Matthew 25:41.
113. Revelation 21:8; 22:15.
114. David L. Edwards and John Stott, *Essentials: A Liberal–Evangelical Dialogue* (Hodder & Stoughton, London, 1988), p. 312.
115. Ibid., p. 314.
116. Matthew 25:46.
117. Revelation 20:10.
118. Revelation 20:15.
119. Mark 16:15.
120. Bible study helps produced by Scripture Union or Inter-Varsity Press.
121. The China Inland Mission, now known as OMF, the Overseas Missionary Fellowship, and the Bible and Medical Missionary Fellowship, now Interserve.
122. The Roman Catholics – a prominent feature of Dublin life.
123. 1 Corinthians 15:33–34.
124. 1 Corinthians 3:16.
125. Charles Swindoll, *Dropping Your Guard* (Hodder & Stoughton, London, 1983), p. 127.
126. Dave Tomlinson, *The Post Evangelical* (Triangle, London, 1995), pp. 33–34.
127. Ibid., p. 12.
128. David Shub, *Lenin: a Biography* (Penguin Books, Harmondsworth, 1966).
129. John 13:35.
130. *Believers' Voice of Victory*, March 2000.
131. Psalm 84:11.
132. *God's Prescription for Divine Health* by Gloria Copeland, taken from www.kcm.com.
133. *Prepare to Prosper* by Gloria Copeland, taken from www.kcm.com.
134. Ephesians 1:4; 1 Thessalonians 4:7.
135. Hebrews 12:10–11.
136. Colossians 1:12.

137. Revelation 21:4.

138. *Nine to Five*, 8 October 2001.

139. John 13:8.

140. John 13:14–15.

141. Douglas Groothuis, *Truth Decay* (Inter-Varsity Press, Leicester, 2000), p. 21.

142. The following is taken from a paper written by C. Peter Wagner of the International Spiritual Warfare Network, entitled *Operation Queen's Palace*.

143. *The Sunday Telegraph*, 13 June 1999.

144. Mel Tari, *Like A Mighty Wind* (Coverdale House, London, 1971).

145. *The Telegraph Magazine*, 4 August 2001.

146. Rebecca Brown, *He Came to Set the Captives Free* (Chick Publications, Chino CA, 1986) and *Prepare For War* (ChickPublications, Chino CA, 1987).

147. *Prepare For War*, p. 17.

148. http://www.mcn.org/1/Miracles/.

149. J. I. Packer, *Fundamentalism and the Word of God* (Inter-Varsity Press, London, 1958), p. 148.

150. Ibid.

151. David Pawson, *Is the Blessing Biblical?* (Hodder & Stoughton, London, 1995).

152. Ibid., p. 94.

153. Matthew 24:24.

154. *The Daily Telegraph*, 5 June 2000.

155. Luke 13:1–5.

156. 1 John 8:8.

157. *Time*, 27 December 1999.

158. Matthew 26:11.

159. Luke 6:20–21.

160. Genesis 3:17.

161. Romans 8:20–21.

162. Ephesians 6:12.

163. Richard Wurmbrand, *In God's Underground* (W. H. Allen, London, 1968), p. 9.

164. Isaiah 53:3.

165. 1 Peter 2:23.
166. 1 John 3:16.
167. John 17:18.
168. John 20:21.
169. John 20:22.
170. Romans 5:5.
171. John 13:35.
172. 1 Chronicles 21.
173. *Hidden Peoples 1980*, chart from US Center for World Mission (Pasadena, 1978).
174. 1978 world population: 4,305,403,287. 2002 world population: 6,234,250,387. US Bureau of the Census, International Data Base (http://www.census.gov/ipc/www/worldpop.html).
175. *The Daily Telegraph*, 12 May 2000.
176. J. Hudson Taylor, *Hudson Taylor's 'Retrospect'* (OMF Books, London, 1974), p. 114.
177. See their impressive web page at www.missionfrontiers.com/newslinks/statewe.html.
178. 2 Peter 3:9.
179. Matthew 25:14–30.
180. Slogan of the AD2000 & Beyond Movement.
181. From *Things as They Are* by Amy Carmichael.
182. Mark 16:18.
183. 1 Thessalonians 1:5.
184. *Newsweek*, 1 May 2000.
185. Matthew 5:45.
186. Acts 1:8.
187. Acts 2:43; 5:12; 8:13 etc.
188. Judges 3:1.
189. Luke 1:1.
190. 1 Timothy 5:23.
191. Philippians 1:17.
192. 2 Timothy 2:9.
193. From the personal story written by my mother after her healing.
194. Colossians 1:9, 11 RSV.

195. Richard Wurmbrand, *Tortured for Christ* (Hodder & Stoughton, London, 1967).
196. 2 Corinthians 4:7.
197. Watchman Nee, *Sit Walk Stand* (Tyndale House Publishers, Wheaton, 1977), pp. 73–77.
198. Hebrews 6:12.
199. John 14:13–14.
200. Kenneth Copeland web page, © 1998 Kenneth Copeland Ministries Inc.
201. Matthew 26:39.
202. Gloria Copeland, *And Jesus Healed them All* (KCP Publications, Fort Worth, TX, 1984), pp. 1, 13, 21, 23.
203. Quoted in Gloria Copeland, op. cit., p. 38.
204. Luke 18:1–8.
205. John 11:1–44.
206. Harold S. Kushner, *When bad things happen to good people* (Pan Books, London, 1981).
207. Ibid., p. 10.
208. Ibid., p. 52.
209. Job 8:6.
210. Hebrews 12:2.
211. Karl Marx, Introduction to *A Contribution to the Critique of Hegel's Philosophy of Law* (Deutsch Französische Jahrbücher, 1844).
212. Luke 6:21, 25.
213. Kushner, op. cit., p. 80.
214. Ibid., p. 82.
215. Romans 8:20.
216. Genesis 3:17.
217. Kushner, op. cit., p. 80.
218. Hebrews 4:15.
219. Job 9:2–3.
220. Job 9:32–33.
221. Job 19:25–26. The word 'Defender' is an alternative to 'Redeemer'.
222. Frank Peretti, *This Present Darkness* (Minstrel, Eastbourne, 1989), p. 421.

224 CAN IT BE TRUE?

223. 2 Kings 4:35.
224. *Time*, special issue, 19 November 1999, p. 50.
225. Winifred Foley, in *The Oldie*, May 2000.
226. Matthew 6:19–20.
227. Ephesians 1:4 RSV.
228. Mark 10:30.
229. *The Sunday Telegraph*, 30 April 2000.
230. John 14:19.
231. John 11:25–26.
232. Revelation 1:9.
233. Revelation 6:9.
234. 1 Corinthians 15:55.
235. John Pollock, *Moody without Sankey* (Hodder & Stoughton, London, 1963), p. 270.
236. *Time*, 15 May 2000.
237. *The Soul of Britain*, BBC TV, first shown in July 2000. Professor Richard Dawkins is Professor of the Public Understanding of Science.
238. Found in the June 1999 newsletter of the Mennonite Church Peace and Justice Committee. Retold by James R. Krabill, Mennonite Board of Missions vice president for Mission Advocacy and Communication.
239. Matthew 18:1–4.